ABRAHAM'S LEGACY:

Ancient Wisdom and Modern Reality

D0916630

Published by

New Mind Productions

P. O. Box 5185
Jersey City, NJ 07305

**Copyright © 1988
by Mustafa El-Amin**

ISBN 0-933821 - 15-8

First Edition   November, 1988
Second Printing - May, 1989
Third Printing - July, 1990

Dedication

This work is dedicated to my parents and to the many courageous people who have struggled to bring light, dignity and progress to humanity.

ACKNOWLEDGEMENTS

I would like to acknowledge all of the special people who helped to make this work possible, especially my wife Joanne El-Amin, Sister Najla Fareed, for typing the manuscript, and Brothers Omar Bey Ali, and Ansari Nadir.

TABLE OF CONTENTS

FOREWORD

"ABRAHAM'S LEGACY: ANCIENT WISDOM, AND MODERN REALITY" is a book that is unique in its scope. It contains information of the past that is relevant and applicable to modern reality.

The seekers of Truth are fortunate to have this scholarly work that has been compiled by Mustafa El-Amin, and I am very happy to have this opportunity to introduce this book and highlight some of its virtues. However, in my humble attempt, I will only be doing the reader a small service before he proceeds to delve into this study, in which he will discover its many virtues throughout its reading.

Mustafa El-Amin deals with a wide range of topics that are essential for community life. Some of the many topics cover: Faith, Reasoning, Knowledge, Man's progression towards Truth, and more. The author attempts to encourage the reader to do a bit of intellectual and social reflection, which will assist the reader in dealing with "modern realities".

In showing the progression of Prophet Abraham's faith in Allah, the author points to the fact that man should not give blind allegiance to any concepts. Man should consult his reasoning and ponder on those things that may not be clear to him. Al-Islam appeals to man's intellect. The followers of Al-Islam should not feel that they can see their way through this religion soley on the basis of blind faith, rather that we should see our way through this religion by the use of intellect.

It was Abraham's curiosity that led him to proper worship. It is the use of intellect that will aid the seeker of Truth to understand modern problems and deal with the challenges of reality.

This book should be of great interest to every student of life, for the author highlights two major concerns: "FAITH and REASONING". It is a high degree of faith and reasoning, along with hard work, that will afford us the opportunity to establish ourselves as individuals and communities worthy of respect. This book will allow the reader the opportunity to utilize the great wisdom of Prophet Abraham's (PBUH) lifestyle in applying it to our modern situations.

One's purpose for studying the past should be to become more aware of the state of the present, leading into the workings of a better future. The great wisdom of the past should influence our efforts of reshaping the present.

It is my earnest hope that this book will excite the hopes of the reader to carefully study the life of Prophet Abraham (PBUH), who represents a high degree of faith and reasoning. I also pray to Allah (Highly Glorified is He), that He will bless this effort with His Mercy, Forgiveness, and Acceptance.

Abdul Khabir Shamsid-Deen,
September 6, 1988

INTRODUCTION

"Abraham was indeed a model, Devoutly obedient to ALLAH (GOD) (and) true in faith, and he joined not gods with God" (16:120 - 123).

Prophet Abraham/Ibrahim is considered to be the "Father of the Faithful" by Christians, Jews and Muslims. His unquestionable faith, obedience and devotion to the Creator is greatly admired by all people of faith. Although there may be differences among the religious communities in regards to Abraham's "religion" there is unity and agreement in regards to his devotional nature. Who can blame anyone for wanting to claim such a man of nobility, integrity, excellence and reasoning. Nevertheless, the Holy Qur'an makes it clear that, "Abraham was not a Jew nor yet a Christian; but he was true in Faith and bowed his will to God's (which is Islam) and he joined not gods with ALLAH." (Sura 5 Ayat 67). The Qur'an also says that Abraham left his sons a legacy in which he instructed them to adhere to the religion of Islam. His words were, "Oh my sons! God hath chosen The Faith for you; then die not except in the Faith of Islam." (Surah 2 Ayat 132).

Abraham, a man of faith, also reflected and demonstrated a sincere desire for knowledge. Abraham was also a man of reason and logic. He was a thinker. His faith led him to knowledge and his knowledge increased his faith. There were some specific events that occurred in the life of Abraham which deserve close scrutiny and review by men and women of faith. These events highlight the importance of faith and knowledge. Some of the events in the life of Abraham not only highlight the great wisdom of the Ancient Masters, but they also provide solutions for our modern reality.

CHAPTER 1

ABRAHAM: THE STARS, THE MOON, AND THE SUN

Abraham was a man who sought answers. He searched inwardly and outwardly for truths. It appears that Abraham had a natural desire to worship a superior and Supreme being. The Holy Qur'an gives a picture of Abraham that leads us to see him as a thinker and a man of faith and inquisition. Because of this he was guided and blessed with understanding.

The Holy Qur'an says, *"So also did we show Abraham the power and the laws of the heavens and the earth that he might (with understanding) have certitude"* (6:75). Think about this! Abraham was given knowledge (shown) of the power and the law of the heavens and the earth. Science tells us that the heavenly bodies, particularly the sun, moon and stars, have an attracting power or pull on the earth. In fact it is the sun's rays that strike the earth and causes it to spin or rotate. This rotation creates what is called centrifugal force or gravity. This gravity actually works as a law. It keeps everything on the earth. It is referred to as the "Law of Gravity". That is only one example of the power of the sun. The sun is so powerful that it keeps our solar system in place. Each planet is in a certain order or atmosphere because of its relationship to the sun. The moon reflects the light of the sun and it has an attraction and effect on the waters of the earth. Perhaps it was some of these things about the heavens and the earth that ALLAH showed Abraham.

It appears that the heavenly bodies as well as the earth follows a calculated and consistent pattern. Evidently ALLAH showed this to Abraham, and in doing so Abraham received understanding which made him stronger in his faith. The Qur'an says ALLAH did not only show him the power but also the laws "that he might (with understanding) have certitude".

1

ALLAH explains the consistent movement and pattern of the heavenly bodies and how the moon follows the sun in a disciplined manner. In Sura 91 of the Holy Qur'an it states, "*By the Sun and his (glorious) splendour; By the Moon as she follows him...*" In Sura 31 Ayat 29 it states, "*He has subjected the sun and the moon (to His Law), each running its course for a term appointed...*"

ABRAHAM: GUIDED TO PROPER WORSHIP

In the above explanation we see that Abraham was given understanding and that he realized that there was a Creator, a Supreme power, that was greater than him. Abraham was a natural man and he reflects the natural development and progression towards truth. ALLAH tells us in the Qur'an that he raises us degree by degree and stage by stage. In Abraham we see that process. He is an excellent example of the human being's growth in knowledge and truth. If we examine what the Qur'an says we will see this clearly.

First Abraham is guided to the point where he learns some things about creation. This led him to the understanding that there was a Supreme Creator. "He might (with understanding) have certitude." What happens after this? He wanted to find ALLAH (GOD). His desire to know ALLAH (GOD) better increased. How do we know this? Because the Holy Qur'an says in the following verse of Sura 6 (Ayat 76) that during the night he looked at the stars and said it was God, he looked at the moon and said it was God, then during the day he looked at the sun and said it was God, and lastly he concluded that the power behind all of them was ALLAH (GOD).

These were the same heavenly objects that ALLAH used to give him understanding. Concerning Abraham's search, The Qur'an specifically says, "*When the night covered him over, he saw a star: He said "This is my Lord." But when it set, He said: I love not those who set' When he saw the moon rising in splendour, He said: "This is my Lord." But when the moon set, He said: "Unless my Lord guide me, I shall surely be among those who go astray." When he saw the sun rising in splendour, He said "This is my Lord; This is the greatest (of all)." But when the sun set, He said "O my people! I am (now) free from your (guilt) of giving partners to ALLAH. For me, I have set my face, firmly and truly, towards Him Who created the heavens and the earth, and never shall I give partners to ALLAH".* (Sura 6 Ayat 76-79).

In reflecting on this event in the life of Abraham we find profound wisdom and encouragement to think, reason and seek knowledge. Muslims know that their religion is after the order of Abraham. The Order of Muhammad is after the "order of Abraham", the "upright in faith". Abraham sought knowledge and understanding. Prophet Muhammad said, "seek wisdom from cradle to grave." It is reported that he also said that "one learned believer gives a greater fight to Satan than thousands of ignorant followers" and that "the ink of the scholar is more holier than the blood of the martyr".

After Abraham learnt that there was a Creator, he wanted to know the Creator better. The more man learns, the more he wants to learn. For example, once a person consciously becomes a Muslim and declares that there is no god but ALLAH and Muhammad is the Messenger, he then is required to learn how to better serve the Creator, and practice the religion. If he is really motivated, he will constantly want to know more and more about his Lord. The more we learn of the mercy, power, compassion and wisdom of ALLAH the better prepared we will become, the more praise we will give to Him, and less praise we will give to other things.

Abraham is an example of the rational urge in man. Although he was a Prophet and the first conscious Muslim, he can also be seen as a model of what occurs in the human being. ALLAH says in the Qur'an that man grows from weakness to strength, and it is He (ALLAH) who brings us from darkness to light. As we grow from a child to adulthood, we may experience various things. For example, we may see our mother as the most

3

superior being because we depend on her for love, warmth, food, etc. Without her perhaps we would not have survived. In fact the first and most crucial years of the child's life are to be spent with the mother. The mother plays the major role in the life of the child at first. Later in life the child grows up to realize that the father is the stronger and more influential parent in the house. He learns for example that as his mother was responsible for maintaining and protecting him, that someone was/is responsible for maintaining and protecting his mother. He finds out what ALLAH revealed in the Qur'an, "*Men are the protectors and maintainers of women, because ALLAH has given them more (strength) than the other, and because they support them from their means. Therefore, the righteous women are devoutly obedient, and guard in (the husband's) absence what ALLAH would have them guard.*" (Sura 4 Ayat 34).

After we grow a little older and mature, we may come to realize that there is something that is bigger and more consuming than both mother and father. The society itself. The society has laws that are designed to protect and maintain the individual life. The society and its leadership is then seen as the authority in the human being's life. And unless we come to realize that there is an all-wise and powerful Creator, who gives life and causes death, we may go on thinking and believing that our fate and destiny rest with the controlling factors of society. We will think that because we live in a Christian society our fate is determined by the Christians, or if it is a communist society, or socialist, or capitalist, or a Jewish society that the realization of our hopes and aspirations are in their hands. No! If ALLAH (GOD) blesses us we will conclude, like Abraham concluded, that the power behind all life is the one we should fear and worship. At some point, whatever else we put our total hope and faith in, will let us down. The only thing that we can put our total faith in is ALLAH.

We too, like Abraham, may have looked at three things (Mother, Father and society) because of their role in our life and because at certain points in our growth they were the greater. That natural process creates in us a sense of appreciation so that once we come to know the real God, we will already know how to show some sense of appreciation towards him. Abraham's experience can also serve as a hint to let us know that perhaps we should be more patient with those who may not have yet been guided to the proper concept of God. If we think about it, most of us at some point worshipped something that was inferior.

In our conclusion on this particular section we would just like to draw the readers attention to a few other important points. Man, society and creation at large grows from smallness to greatness, from little to big. The human being grows from a small leech-like creature to a full grown six-foot human being. Society grows from a small family to a large nation. The Qur'an says Abraham first saw the smallest object in the heavens at night. The stars appear smaller than the moon. After that, he looked at the moon which appears larger than the stars but is smaller than the sun. Lastly, he looked at what appears to be the largest object in the universe, the sun. Shouldn't this make us raise certain questions and think.

What is it telling us? I believe it is reminding us of the natural growth from inferior to superior. From smallness to greatness. It is not likely that Abraham had never seen the sun or the moon before he saw the star. If he did see the sun before he saw the star and moon, he would have realized that it had more splendor and was brighter. Evidently, the sequence is very, very important. ALLAH is All wise and his method of guiding and instructing is so profound until sometimes it requires deep thought and reflection to gain a real appreciation of it. We may say, for example, "the sun, moon and star". ALLAH says, "star, moon and sun". We may say, "day and night" whereas in some places in the Qur'an ALLAH says, "He causes the day to follow the night..." (Sura 31 Ayat 29). The Qur'an also says ALLAH leads us from darkness to light (Sura 5 Ayat 18). The Christian Bible says, "The Evening and the Morning" (Genesis). Abraham's search began at night. Prophet Muhammad received the first revelation of the Qur'an at night, and at a time when his people were steeped in mental and moral darkness. Abraham's people were also enslaved in ignorance. They worshipped idols that they had carved out with their own hands. Abraham was brought to the

5

light of understanding during a time when his people groped in darkness.

It is interesting to note that as ALLAH tells us in the Qur'an, Abraham looked at the star first, the moon second, and the sun third. ALLAH revealed to Prophet Muhammad sura's under the title of each of these heavenly objects and they are arranged in the same order:

Najm (The Star) Sura 53
Qamar (The Moon) Sura 54
Sham (The Sun) Sura 91.

Each of these suras, like all the rest, must be very important, particularly as they relate to the story of Abraham. It may be helpful to the reader when reciting the ayats on Abraham to also consider what the above suras say of the stars, moon and sun. Let us consider some of the characteristics and functions of each of these objects. It is reported that Prophet Muhammad told his enemies that if they gave him the sun in his right hand and the moon in his left he would not stop teaching the message of Islam.

CHAPTER 2

THREE GREAT LIGHTS

Abraham's growth towards the right concept of ALLAH (GOD) was a natural progression. Remember The Order of the Prophet Muhammad is in line with the Order of Abraham. Each object that Abraham looked at gives light. This could mean that Abraham first received a little light, then he received more light (the moon appears to be brighter than the stars). Then he received much more light (the sun, the brightest of all). Lastly, he received the truth, the sure Reality. But that came about through a gradual stage by stage development. Let us turn our attention to a brief discussion of the three great lights.

THE STARS

The Qur'an makes various statements about the stars. Science tells us that many stars are as big as the sun and that their energy radiates or generates from within. The stars have long been used as a guide for the navigator. However, it appears as though the stars go into hiding during the day. The stars are of little use during the day. Their greatest benefit is during the night. They represent hope during a time of darkness. In fact, the Bible says that God promised Abraham that his seeds would be like the stars in heaven (Gen.15:5). The Bible also says there was a star in the east during the time of Jesus's birth and it served as a guide to the wise men who came bearing gifts. The Eastern Stars say, "I have seen his star in the East and have come to worship him." Star gazing is an ancient practice. Metaphysically speaking, stars represent enlightened thoughts and ideas. Dr. Maurice Bucaille explains "..... the stars are heavenly bodies like the Sun. They are the scene of various physical phenomena of which the easiest to observe is their generation of light. They are heavenly bodies that produce their own light". (The Bible, The Qur'an and Science, page 165).

7

He also points out that the word star appears thirteen times in the Qur'an. It states:

• *"He created The Sun, The Moon, and The Stars (all) governed by laws under His command." (7:54).*

• *"...and The Stars are in subjection by His command: Verily in this are signs for men who are wise." (16:12).*

• *"...And by the stars (Men) guide themselves." (16:16).*

• *"Seest thou not that to ALLAH bow down in worship all things that are in the heavens and on earth, The Sun, The Moon, The Stars...." (22:18).*

• *"We have indeed decked the lower heaven with beauty (in) the stars" (37.6).*

• *"Then when the stars become dim..." (77:8).*

• *"When the stars fall, losing their lustre" (81:2).*

• *"When the stars are scattered" (82:2).*

• *"By the star when it goes down - your companion is neither astray nor being misled. (53:1,2).*

• *"By the Sky and the Night-Visitant (Therein): And what will explain to thee what the Night Visitant is? (It is) the Star of piercing brightness." (86: 1-3).*

The stars are very important to us. They have great significance in the physical creation and profound meaning in the spiritual and metaphysical sciences.

THE MOON

The moon is not a light in itself, it reflects the sunlight upon the earth. The moon does not project light nor does it originate its own light. The moon is like a balance or equalizer between the sun and the earth. Science tells us that the moon has an attracting pull on the waters. It draws the water up into the sky where the water condenses and forms clouds. After a period of time, and with the changing of temperature in the atmosphere, the water rains back down on the earth. It should be noted, however, that once the water forms into clouds most times they travel (are moved by the wind) from a wet fertile area to a dry distill area that needs water. It then de-condenses and returns to the earth in the form of rain. The Holy Qur'an mentions this sophisticated process several times:

> "And We send the fecundating winds, then cause the rain to descend from the sky, therewith providing you with water...." (15:22)

> "It is ALLAH (GOD) Who sends forth the winds, so that they raise up the clouds and We drive them to a land that is dead, and revive the earth therewith, after its death...." (35:9)

> "It is ALLAH Who sends the winds, and they raise the clouds; then does He spread them in the sky as He wills, and breaks them into fragments, until thou seest rain drops issue from the midst thereof...." (30:48)

The moon does not only affect the streams, the lakes, the rivers and oceans, it also has an impact on human beings. The Qur'an and modern science say that we are created or formed in water: "It is He Who has created man from water." (25:54). It is also a matter of fact that the human body is composed of approximately 60 to 90 percent water. Therefore, it is reasonable to conclude that the moon is very important to us as physical beings also. At certain times the moon disturbs the waters, and at

9

other times it leaves them calm and peaceful. It is also believed that the moon affects our moods and emotional behavior. The moon waxes and wanes through the sky; as it travels and rotates, it appears as though it is changing form. The moon is always round or circular. It only appears different because of its relationship to the earth at various times of the month. The moon has long been used as a means of calculating time.

The Qur'an says, "*It is He Who made the sun to be a shinning glory and the moon to be a light (of beauty), and measured out stages for her; that ye might know the number of years and the count of (time)...*" (10:5). For example, the Muslim world uses what is called the Lunar calendar, whereas the Western world uses the Solar calendar to designate the various months and years. The beginning and ending of the Muslim's fast (Ramadan) is based on the sighting of the moon. Both Eid-ul-Fitr and Eid-Ul-Adha are associated with the sighting of the moon.

ALLAH also tells us in the Qur'an that the moon and the creation itself is a sign. The sky or heavens are sometimes associated with the spiritual. Often times when people think of heaven or the after-life, the spiritual reality, they tend to look up toward the sky. Abraham looked to the sky. Prophet Muhammad also looked to the sky for Qibla, or direction: "*We see the turning of thy face (for guidance) to the heavens...*" (H. Q. 2:144).

The moonlight allows us to see what is in the sky at night. It does not help our vision much on earth. So, for example, a person who travels a dark road or walks a pathway during the night cannot depend on the moonlight alone to help him see. He will need a flashlight to help him avoid the ditch or pitfalls on the road. Therefore, the moon is not usually referred to as a symbol of material vision and awareness, as much as it is a spiritual one. The moon shows us the beautiful canopy of heaven. It helps us to see the various star formations, the Milky Way, et cetera. The moon is a symbol of heavenly or spiritual vision and spiritual logic.

Concerning the moon the Qur'an states:

"They ask thee concerning the New Moons, Say: They are but signs to mark fixed periods of time in (the affairs of) men, and for pilgrimage." (2:189)

"Blessed is the One Who placed the constellations in heaven and placed therein a lamp and a moon giving light." (25:61)

"Did you see how ALLAH created seven heavens one above another and made the moon a light therein and made the sun a lamp?" (71:15 -16)

"The Hour (of Judgement) is nigh, and the moon is cleft asunder" (54:1)

The observation and study of the moon reveals a wealth of knowledge and it is indeed a thought-provoking sign. Although it is by no means an object for worship, it is a very important symbol and a reality in the life of man and creation. Through Abraham we get the understanding, that it should be looked at, studied and examined, but not worshipped as God. No matter how important a thing may be in our life, if we look at it and study it long enough, as Abraham did, we will find some flaws, some errors which will let us know that these things are not ALLAH (GOD).

THE SUN

The sun is a ball of energy that generates its own light. It projects light throughout our solar system. The sun is essential to human life. The sun pulls and attracts the life that is on earth. Its magnetic pull contributes to the growth of human, animal and plant life. The sun does not only provide us with light and warmth but it gives us vitamins that are needed to sustain life. The sun is a source of great utility to man. The Holy Qur'an states: *"Do ye-not see that GOD has subjected to your (use) all things in the heavens, and on earth, and has made His bounties flow to you in exceeding measure, (both) seen and unseen?"* (31:20)

The sun causes the dead seed that is placed into the earth to grow and burst forth into the open environment. The plant reaches towards the sun because it receives energy and substance from the sun. This is called photosynthesis. The sun raises the dead. Its rays sets the earth in motion and activity. The sun has an affect on the entire earth. The sun is consistent. We can always count on the sun to rise in the east and set in the west. It travels through the heavens. Imam W. D. Muhammad explained, "The heaven is the most impressive sign of obedience that God wants from His creature. The sun rises in the morning, it sets at night. It does that day after day after day.... It has definite movement. It graces the East, it graces the West on the horizon and also on the horizon of its setting. Over the year it will make a bow to the north and a bow to the south; so ALLAH says He is the Lord of the two Easts and the two Wests." (Los Angeles, November 15, 1987).

Because the sun gives freely of itself it has also been symbolized as a sign of freedom and leadership. It rules the heavens. The Bible says, "And God made two great lights; the greater light to rule the day." (Genesis 1:16). True leadership feeds and nourishes the mind just like the sun feeds and nourishes the creation. True leadership gives light and knowledge so that man can see, think, and walk upright upon the earth. True leadership is not selfish, it gives to all. True leadership tries to pull man up from a low, lifeless condition to an active, dignified posture. True leadership creates a climate that will be conducive for mental, moral and spiritual growth and development. True leadership, like the sun, bows and obeys the laws of the Creator.

The sun is a marvelous creation. It is part of the handiwork of ALLAH (GOD). It is a Muslim. So dear reader, let us consider with deeper thought what is meant when it is said that "Abraham looked at the sun". Let us consider the fact that although he should not have worshipped it as ALLAH, he did in fact gain great wisdom and use from his observation. In fact, it was the setting of the sun, according to the Holy Qur'an, that caused Abraham to come to the realization that the Lord and Cherisher, the Creator of the Sun, Moon and Stars, was the ALLAH (GOD) that he should be worshipping. Abraham looked at something that was bigger than himself. The Qur'an says, "*Assuredly the creation of the heavens and the earth is a greater (matter) than the creation of men: yet most men understand not.*" (40:57). We should respect leadership, and those who may have a greater or bigger responsibility in the world than we do. It is intelligent to study and observe their actions and behavior. However, no matter how much light they may give, we should never ever worship them as ALLAH (GOD). The Western world is extremely guilty of leading us to believe in and worship an anthropomorphic concept of God. Leadership is vitally necessary in the life of man and society, but it should be kept in the right perspective. It is reported that Prophet Muhammad said: "Religion is sincerity to ALLAH and His Book, and His Messenger, and to the leaders of the Muslim and their common folk." (Related by Muslim).

Not only is the sun important as a sign of leadership, but its function also inculcates a metaphysical message that alludes to material and rational vision. The Sun, unlike the moon, shows us clearly what is on the material earth. The sun enables us to see what is down here on the physical ground. The earth is more material than it is space. Space is non material. The sky or heaven appears to be more spacious than the earth. In fact, it is called "space." We say the astronauts travelled to outer space. The sky is associated with the spiritual and the earth refers to the material. As we mentioned, the sun shows or reveals what is on the earth more so than it reveals what is in the sky or heavens. In fact, the day seems to conceal what is in the heavens and reveals what is on the earth. Reflect! Think! When we look up in the sky during the day, we don't see the beautiful star formations, the planets, et cetera. During the day the sky looks like a blank piece of paper. It looks like nothing is there. The sun does not show us the spiritual operation, therefore, the Bible and the Qur'an tell us the great Prophets and Messengers received their spiritual vision and insight during the night.

The moon shows man the heaven, therefore it symbolizes spiritual vision, and the sun symbolizes material vision. Man needs both, the night and the day, the sun and the moon. ALLAH highlights this fact in these words: *"Seest thou not that ALLAH (GOD) merges Night into Day and He merges Day into Night..."* (31:29). The Qur'an also says *"...He makes the Night overlap the day, and the day overlap the night."* (39:5). The Islamic fast, the Hajj, and the Eids are related to the moon or the night, whereas our five obligatory prayers are associated with the sun. The sun has always held a high place in the life of ancient and modern man. ALLAH revealed a complete sura to Prophet Muhammad called Al-Sham (The Sun): *"By the Sun and his (glorious) splendour; By the Moon as she follows him; By the day as it shows up (the Sun's) glory; By the Night as it conceals it; By the Firmament and its (wonderful) structure; By the Earth and its (wide) expanse; By the Soul, and the proportion and order given to it; And its enlightenment as to its wrong and its right; Truly he succeeds that purifies it, and he fails that corrupts it . . . . . "* (91:1-10).

CHAPTER 3

ABRAHAM REJECTS FALSE WORSHIP: TRIES TO EDUCATE HIS PEOPLE

Also mentioned in the Book, the story of Abraham: He was a man of Truth, a prophet:

"Behold, he said to his father: "Oh my father! Why worship that which heareth not and seeth not, and can profit thee nothing? O my father! to me hath come knowledge which hath not reached thee: So follow me: I will guide thee to a way that is even and straight. O my father! serve not Satan: for Satan is a rebel against (ALLAH) Most Gracious. O my father! I fear lest a penalty afflict thee from (ALLAH) Most Gracious, so that thou become to Satan a friend." (The father) replied: Dost thou hate my gods, O Abraham? If thou forbear not, I will indeed stone thee: Now get away from me for a good long while! Abraham said: "Peace be on thee: I will pray to my Lord for thy forgiveness: For He is to me Most Gracious. And I will turn away from you (all) and from those whom ye invoke besides ALLAH: I will call on my Lord: Perhaps, by my prayer to my Lord, I shall be not unblest." (H.Q. 19:41 - 48).

After Abraham learned of the true God, ALLAH, he rejected all forms of idol worship. Abraham then went to his people and tried to educate them and call them away from idol worship. This shows us that Abraham was not only a man of faith and reason, but he also "desired for his brother what he desired for himself." He had a charitable nature and he wanted the people to be enlightened. He tried to get them to think, to use their intelligence. He appealed to their rational mind. The Qur'an says that one day Abraham destroyed all of their idols except one. The Qur'an goes on to say that when they returned and asked Abraham who had destroyed their idols he answered them with a loaded, but thought-provoking statement. According to the Qur'an

15

Abraham said, "ask the biggest one!" In other words, if he is the God then surely he can at least tell you who destroyed the other idols. They responded by saying, "you know they cannot speak".

One would think that, that profound act would have caused them to realize how ignorant they were to worship an idol. The fact of the matter is that you can give a person sound, concrete, logical and rational reasons why they should or should not do something, but because of their emotional or passionate involvement they will not accept what you say. Nevertheless, we should still make the initial effort. We should always share the precious knowledge that God gives us. Abraham did not learn about the true God and then keep it to himself. He was not selfish.

The Holy Qur'an explains in several places how Abraham tried to enlighten his people: The Qur'an states:

"Low! Abraham said to his father Azar, 'Takest thou idols for gods? For I see thee and thy people in manifest error'." (6:74).

"His people disputed with him. He said: "(Come) ye to dispute with me, about ALLAH, when He (Himself) hath guided me? I fear not (the beings) ye associate with ALLAH: Unless my Lord willeth, (nothing can happen). My Lord comprehendeth in his knowledge all things: Will ye not (yourselves) be admonished?" (6:80)

"What was the reasoning, about us. which we gave to Abraham (To Use) against his people: We raise whom We will, degree after degree: For thy Lord is full of wisdom and knowledge." (6.83)

"We bestowed aforetime on Abraham his rectitude of conduct, and well were We acquainted with him. Behold! he said to his father and his people, "What are these images to which ye are (so assiduously) devoted?" They said, "We found our fathers worshipping them." He said, "indeed ye have been in manifest error—ye and your fathers." They said, "Have you brought the

Truth, or are you one of those who jest? He said, "Nay, your Lord is the Lord of the heavens and the earth, He who created them (from nothing): And I am a witness to this (truth)." (21:51-56).

"And rehearse to them (something of) Abraham's story. Behold, he said to his father and his people: "What worship ye?" They said: "We worship Idols, and we remain constantly in attendance on them." He said: "Do they listen to you when ye call (on them), or do you good or harm?" (26:70-73)

"And (we also saved) Abraham: Behold, he said to his people, "Serve God and fear Him: that will be best for you - If ye understand!" (29:16)

Abraham loved his father and his people, however, he did not allow that to keep him from telling them the truth.

Sometimes our emotional attachment to a person may cause us to avoid telling them the truth out of fear of hurting their feelings. In Abraham we also see an exemplification of the Qur'anic statement, "*O ye who believe fear ALLAH alone and always speak a word direct to the right.*"

A RATIONAL APPEAL

Not only did Abraham proclaim the message he had received, but he also debated with the people. He presented sound and logical arguments. He didn't just make an emotional appeal. He addressed their intellect with the principals of reasoning. He made a rational appeal. During a debate with a particular skeptic Abraham demonstrated his keen use of logic and his profound ability to address the rational mind. The Qur'an draws our attention to this event: "*Hast thou not turned thy vision to one who disputed with Abraham about his Lord, because ALLAH had granted him power? Abraham said: "My Lord is He who giveth life and death". He said: "I give life and death." Said Abraham: "But it is ALLAH that causeth the sun to rise from the East. Do thou then cause him to rise from the West. " Thus was he*

17

confounded who (in arrogance) rejected Faith. Nor doth ALLAH give guidance to a people unjust." (3:2 58).

Abraham was prudent and wise. If we contemplate on Abraham and examine what the Qur'an says of him, perhaps we will devote more time to developing rational arguments to use in our dawah (propagation) efforts. The Christian church, particularly the leadership, has been guilty of bypassing the rational intelligence of the people and appealing only to their emotional nature. Abraham did not do that. The Jewish community in regarding itself as some special and chosen creature of God, has totally abandoned any evangelical efforts. For the most part the Jewish community does not attempt to teach or share the precious knowledge with anyone who is not "Jewish." Abraham did not conceal the knowledge. History shows us however, that the true Muslim tried and is still trying to educate the masses of people. The Muslim took the precious message of Islam throughout the earth. Therefore, the Qur'an says of Abraham: *"Abraham was not a Jew nor yet a Christian, but he was true in Faith, and bowed his will to ALLAH'S (which is Islam) and he joined not gods with ALLAH"* (3:67). It is essential for us to have genuine taqwa (love and respect for God) if we are to be successful in our propagation efforts. Abraham had genuine taqwa and because of that, ALLAH protected him. ALLAH saved his life. Yes, there are people who will try to kill you physically, mentally and spiritually for teaching the truth. The enemies of humanity will do all they can to stop the masses of people from getting the precious knowledge. The Qur'an tells us that Abraham was cast into a furnace of fire because he tried to bring his people from darkness to light.

CHAPTER 4

ABRAHAM CAST INTO THE FIRE

"They said burn him and protect your gods, if ye do
(anything at all)." (21:68)

"They said, "Build him a furnace and throw him into
the blazing fire!" (37:97)

Abraham was so committed to educating his people until
he devised a plan that involved the destruction of their idol gods.
According to the story Abraham said, "*And by ALLAH I have a
plan for your idols.... So he broke them to pieces, (all) but the
biggest of them, that they might turn (and address themselves to
it).*" (21:57, 58). Consequently, an intense dialogue took place
between Abraham and the worshippers of the idol gods.
According to the Qur'an, when they questioned Abraham, he said
"*Nay, this was done by the biggest one! Ask them, if they can
speak intelligently!*" (21: 63). The idol worshipers responded by
saying, "*Thou knowest full well that these (idols) do not speak!*"
Abraham then challenged the logic of their worship, he said "*Do
ye then worship, besides ALLAH, things that can neither be of
any good to you nor do you harm?..... Have ye no sense?*" (21:
66,67). According to the story they felt a sense of shame.
However, their pride and their ignorance would not allow them to
submit and humble themselves. Quite the contrary, they became so
arrogant and hostile until they took the time and energy to build a
firery furnace specifically to burn Abraham. (37: 97).

Let us bear in mind that although these people were
ignorant of the true God, that they did have a considerable amount
of secular knowledge. They were environmentally wise. Abraham
was born in Mesopotamia (now called Iraq). The people of
Mesopotamia were known for their intelligence, writing ability,
eloquence and artistry. Rudolph R. Windsor explains "More than

6,000 years ago in the land called Mesopotamia there developed the most remarkable civilization then known to mankind. This civilization was centered between the Tigris and the Euphrates Rivers. This southern section was known at different times by many names, among which are Sumer, Akkad, and Chaldea; but the name best known to us is Babylonia. This area was also the location of the Garden of Eden and the people of this region were jet black." (From Babylon To Timbuktu page 13). However, because their idea of God was incorrect, they thought they could make God and protect God. They had various ideas about God. The proof of this is that they made different types, sizes and shapes of idols. Some had a small idea of God so they made a small god. Those who had a big idea of God made a big idol.

Abraham, therefore was also trying to destroy false ideas and foolish thinking. Ideas are greater and more significant than physical images. In fact the image is a reflection or manifestation of the thought. It can be concluded then that Abraham did not only destroy the physical idols, but he also destroyed the false concepts. The Holy Qur'an says he destroyed them with his right hand (which is the strongest hand): *"Then did he turn upon them, striking (them) with his right hand"* (37: 93). The right hand is usually the most dominant, and it refers to strength and conscience. The Qur'an said Moses carried his staff in his right hand, Muslims place their right hand over their left during prayer (Qiyam or standing position). At the end of the prayer, Muslims turn first to the right and say As-Salaam Alaikum wa rahmatullah.

Perhaps Abraham in destroying the idols with his right hand refers to his strong conscious appeal to the people and a sign to us that we should use strong arguments that address the conscience. It seems that Abraham made the first appeal from the right, just as the Muezzin (Prayer Caller) makes the first appeal or call from the right when he says "come to prayer" twice. Brothers and Sisters, we should appeal to the good conscience of the people. Abraham's argument was superior than the false ideas of the people. Destroying the idols may mean overcoming or defeating the false inferior ideas with truth and superior knowledge. Defeating the idea does not guarantee that all of the

20

people will submit. An example of this is the story of Moses. He defeated Pharoah's sorcerers, scholars, magicians, etc., and although they submitted, the King and his army did not. In fact they attempted to kill Moses just as the leaders of Mesopotamia tried to kill Abraham.

THE BIGGEST ONE

Abraham destroyed all of the idols or ideas except for the biggest one. He did this when the leaders were not present, when their backs were turned. (H. Q. 21:57). It is reported that he told the leaders of the idol worshippers (when they returned and faced him) to ask the biggest one to tell them who destroyed the smaller ones. They responded by saying that the biggest one can not speak. If we can understand the idols as also referring to false, oppressive ideas, then perhaps we can make a closer association of this story with our current situation and responsibilities. As already stated, idols or images that are "carved" by men are usually a reflection of their mind or imagination. An image is the manifestation of an imagination. There is a difference in worshipping something that is beyond your control and that which you make yourself.

The "biggest one" represents the dominant overruling concept or idea of God that existed in that society. For example, here in America the dominant overruling concept or idea of God is the trinity, and that Jesus is God and the son of God. Although there are other ideas and beliefs that exist in America today, they are smaller than that belief. There are those who worship all kinds of false ideas. Nevertheless, those ideas are not as dominant as the Christian idea of Jesus. Abraham destroyed or defeated the false idols or ideas when the leaders were not looking, when their "backs were turned." In other words, they had left the thinking and imagination of the people unattended. They had turned their back on the masses. They had not taught and encouraged the people to think for themselves. They had not given the people the knowledge of the true God. Those people were left without sound principles for their lives. The people were mentally dependent on the false leadership. Percival states, "Democracy is Self

Government." They were not under a true democracy. Their minds were closed, just as Allen Bloom says, the American peoples' minds are closed (The Closing of the American Mind). Abraham went after the unattended masses. He taught the ignorant masses, thus destroying their false concept of God. The Bible says Jesus did the same thing. It says he told his disciples to go and untie the donkey that was unattended.

Abraham was a liberator. He freed the people's mind. He broke the mental chains of superstition and idol worship. He freed them from the slavery or mental oppression and false ideas. That is why the leaders were so upset when they returned. They said, "Who has done this? Who has done this? Let us protect our idol concepts." The leaders knew that the biggest false image or concept did not do it, because the biggest one was a lie itself. Therefore, it could not destroy the other false concepts with truth and free the minds of the people. The biggest one was just a vehicle for containing the masses.

The leaders said "you know the biggest one cannot speak!" This can be understood today, in our modern life time to mean that the big lie and false concept of Jesus as God and that he died on the cross for the sins of the world, cannot speak or does not speak truthfully to the minds of the people. Perhaps, what the leaders were saying to Abraham was that the biggest false concept would not give liberation to the people or destroy the smaller lies. The biggest one was not based on truth. Only truth will make a man free. The Bible says "You shall know the truth and the truth will set you free."

The wise in the leadership of America and the West know that the trinity and the belief that Jesus is God, the son of God, is a big lie. They know it does not speak the truth to the people. That false idea cannot free the people from drugs and alcohol. It cannot stop the people from worshipping immorality, indecency. They know that, that big lie will not kill racism, bigotry and injustice. They know it cannot raise the dead. It cannot give you the courage and the back bone to stand up like a man and meet the challenges of life. They know it really makes you a weak, emotional, helpless

22

sheep. Therefore, when a man stands up and says that, that ideology freed him, the leaders know he is telling a damn lie. White Western false Christianity can never free the masses of people. In fact, it contains and restricts the rational, intelligent operation of the mind. The leaders of the western world do not believe and accept the teachings of Christianity in the same way they encourage the masses to. They have a higher, more profound idea of Christ, God, and the trinity.

Returning to Abraham now, we can understand then that perhaps what the leaders were saying to Abraham was this, "We know this idea will not liberate the people. This is an idea that is used to enslave the people. We know, Abraham, that it did not speak to them. It did not speak to their intelligence, their soul, their heart and their good nature to make them give up their false idea of God. We know that, Abraham. We only have that false idea in place as a means of keeping the people in check; but in our secret, higher, elitest order we have a brighter, better and superior concept of God." Nowadays the leaders are probably saying, "We have a superior concept that is even greater than the idea that God manifests himself in Jesus Christ. We have a better idea of the trinity. We don't believe in the God the father, the son and the holy ghost. We know that the trinity refers to the physical, mental, and spiritual nature of man, but we won't tell the masses, because it may cause them to start thinking right."

Once the leaders realize that you have peeped their game, like Abraham did, then they come out with some of their higher firery wisdom. They try to test you with their best to see if you really have the goods. They turn the heat up on you. The Holy Qur'an says they cast Abraham into the fire.

THE FIRE

The story says that Abraham was protected in the fire. "*We said, 'O Fire! Be thou cool and (a means of) safety for Abraham.*" (21:69). Fire has a dual nature, like most things in creation. It can be used positively or negatively. It can be useful or destructive.

When fire is controlled, when it has parameters or boundaries, it burns very peacefully. On the other hand, when fire rages out of control it brings death and destruction to man and creation. ALLAH says He has given us fire as a benefit and a convenience: "*See ye the Fire which ye kindle?" We have made it a memorial (of Our handiwork), and an article of comfort and convenience for the denizens of deserts."* (56:71,73). Moses, according to Scripture, was able to get some good use from fire. It is reported that he received guidance from the burning bush. The Holy Qur'an states, "*Behold, he saw a fire: So he said to his family, Tarry ye; I perceive a fire; perhaps I can bring you some burning brand therefrom, or find some guidance at the fire. But when he came to the fire, a voice was heard: 'O Moses! Verily I am thy Lord!...*" (20:10-13). The Bible states, "*Now Moses kept the flock of Jethro, his father-in-law, the priest of Median: and he led the flock to the back side of the desert, and came to the mountain of God, even to Herob. And the Angel of the Lord appeared unto him in a flame of fire out of the midst of a bush; and he looked and, behold, the bush burned with fire, and the bush was consumed*" (Exodus 3:12). The Scripture also tells us that fire will be used to punish the wicked and sinful people. "*As to,those who are rebellious and wicked, their abode will be the Fire: every time they wish to get away therefrom, they will be forced thereinto, and it will be said to them: "Taste ye the penalty of the Fire, the which ye were want to reject as false*" (H.Q. 32:20). The Bible states, "*So shall it be at the end of the world: the angels shall come forth, and sever the wicked from among the just, and shall cast them into the furnace of fire: there shall be wailing and gnashing of teeth.*" (Matthew 13:49-50).

The Qur'an says Moses received guidance and inspiration by fire, and that Abraham found peace and safety in the fire. This tells us then that there are some other possibilities that we should consider when reading about the life of Abraham and the fact that he was placed in the fire. The Holy Qur'an is clear, and we must accept what it says. If it says Abraham was placed in a furnace of fire and ALLAH protected him from being burnt, then we must accept that. ALLAH says it is a sign for those who believe (29:24).

Let us, for the sake of understanding, consider some other points. Fire disintegrates matter. It breaks the material down to its primary or elementary stage. Fire reduces matter to its original form. Fire also purifies. Fire is associated with anger, passion, anarchy and wisdom. Because of the heat that it generates, it is also associated with hostility. When a person is angry his temperature rises, his pulse beats faster, generally he gets very excited and is prone to react very emotionally. As a result he may bring harm and danger to an innocent person. An angry person may rage out of control like fire. His passions may lead him to do things that he may not other wise have done. Therefore, the Prophet Muhammad was moved to say, "Do not get angry." It is reported that a man said to the Prophet Muhammad (PBUH), "Counsel me. He (The Prophet) said: 'Do not become angry'. The man repeated (his request) several times, and he said: 'Do not become angry'" (Bukhari).

Once fire escapes and burns free, it does not stop until it has totally destroyed everything in its path. Fire out of control is like freedom without laws, justice or responsibility. That is anarchy. The Webster Dictionary defines anarchy as: *lawlessness, rulerless, lack of government; a state of society when there is no law or supreme power; uncontrolled political confusion, and disorder.* Fire is like wisdom in that it allows you to see the origin of matter. Wisdom is the understanding of the matter. Wisdom is the understanding of the nature of events. For example a person who has wisdom tries to get the source, the point of origination. Wisdom is generally defined as *the faculty to discern right and truth, and to judge and act accordingly; sound judgement; sagacity; discretion; extensive knowledge.* Wisdom, like fire, is very important in the life of man, In Fact the Holy Qur'an says ALLAH gave Joseph wisdom: "*And when he reached his prime We gave him wisdom and knowledge...*" (12:22). The Qur'an also tells us that Abraham prayed to ALLAH to raise up a messenger who would teach wisdom, "*Our Lord! send amongst them an apostle of their own, who shall rehearse Thy Signs to them and instruct them in Scripture and Wisdom and sanctify them: For Thou art the*

Exalted in Might The Wise." (2:129). Wisdom without prayer and appreciation can lead to arrogance.

Iblis was wise. He was very knowledgeable; but his pride polluted his knowledge and wisdom. Iblis was made of fire. He was made of great wisdom and knowledge. He was so wise until he became the leader over the angels. According to the Qur'an fire is also associated with Iblis, who was very wise. "*God said 'O Iblis! What prevents thee from prostrating thyself to one whom I have created with My hands? Art thou naughty? Or art thou one of the high (and mighty) ones? (Iblis) said: "I am better then he; Thou created me from fire, and him Thou created from clay.*" (38:75,76). Iblis felt that his firery, witty, intellectual nature was better than the human being's submissive and appreciative nature. Clay submits to be molded and fashioned into various shapes. Our minds are very impressionable. The mind is influenced and shaped by its encounter with the environment. Iblis, like uncontrolled fire, said he would destroy man. Satan and his forces have caused much destruction in the life of man and society. In fact it appears that some governments are ruled by Satan.

The idea of fire representing wisdom, an intellectual expression, can also be found in The New Webster Comprehensive Dictionary of the English Language. It gives several definitions: *Fire; a rapid succession, as of questions; liveliness of imagination; severe verbal criticism.* These definitions of fire are related to human intellectual expression. The Bible gives us the same idea. It refers to people who spoke with firery tongues. "And the tongue is a fire" (James 3:6).

Fire is also associated with opposition, trials, tests, challenges and hardship. The heat from fire makes us sweat and thirst. It also makes us weak and tired. Too much heat can kill us. Sometimes we have to protect ourselves from the heat. Ramadan is associated with heat. The fast is a trial. During the fast Muslims are tried by the heat of passions, the heat of thirst, the heat of hunger and even the heat of the physical environment. Some people can endure more heat than others. When a person or group says they are going to "turn the fire up" or "put the heat on", this means they are going to try harder to destroy their opponent. A good example of this is the history of Prophet Muhammad. The Quraish Tribe and the other enemies of the Prophet put extreme heat, in the form of oppression, slaughter and deceit on the Prophet and his followers. ALLAH blessed the Muslims with faith and endurance. They overcame the oppression. There are other examples today. The Muhajirs of Afghanistan, the Palestinians who are being oppressed and slaughtered outright by the Zionist Jews. The Africans of South Africa are under the heat of a racist, devilish and terrorists government.

The African-Americans have been under the heat of slavery, racism, bigotry, injustice, lies and deceit. The fire of hatred has been burning in America for a very long time. Now that we have established that fire has various connotations and meanings, let us return to Abraham in the Fire and look at it in light of various definitions of fire. Insha'Allah, God willing, the reader will get more understanding and appreciation from the story.

Abraham is an excellent model of faith and reason. Therefore, placing him in the fire represents an attempt to destroy the devotional and rational nature in man. The leaders tried to reduce Abraham's faith and reasoning to its elementary and primitive stages. They did not want him to reason on the high plane of dignity, nor did they want him to believe in a higher more advanced concept of God. They wanted to disintegrate it to nothing but ashes. They did not want him to have any stability. Ashes are just the particles of matter. Ashes have no stability, they just go with the wind. Abraham was upright, and he was firmly rooted in the faith. Abraham stood on solid ground. He was convinced of his belief. That is why the fire of oppression, anger, wisdom and passions couldn't destroy him.

This is a sign to us. This tells us that we should be firm and stable in our belief. What gave Abraham stability? Knowledge! The more we learn of our religion the stronger we can become. The Prophet Muhammad said, "One learned Muslim is better than hundreds of ignorant followers." Some of us are like ashes; whichever way the wind blows that is where we go. The evil manipulators of this world do not want us to think and reason on a high dignified plane. They don't want men to uphold the proper faith in ALLAH or reason correctly. Every day these evil leaders of this world try to burn out the minds and hearts of the believers. They want us to go back to pagan, primitive, elementary thinking and worship. They want us to worship man as God. They want us to say, "The Black man is God! The White man is the devil!" or "The White man is God and the Black man is cursed by God!" They want us to give up hope and trust in God and leadership.

Abraham did not bow down and submit to their fire god. He did not capitulate. We can also understand this to mean that Abraham was able to stand up against the wisest leadership of his day. After Abraham had defeated all of the other gods, idols, ideologies and philosophies, he was challenged by those of wisdom. As we mentioned, fire represents a severe critical argument. Therefore, we can understand it to mean that they came against him with their religious or philosophical arguments. In other words, they brought out the heavy weights in knowledge. They came with their secret, esoteric knowledge. The Qur'an says this is what pharaoh did with Moses and Aaron. Pharaoh said, "*Bring me every sorcerer well versed*". (10:79).

Just as they were defeated by Moses and Aaron, so were they defeated by Abraham. The Qur'an says ALLAH made the fire cool and peaceful. The Qur'an also says Iblis or Satan is a creature of fire. ALLAH told Iblis that he could not deceive His servants. Abraham was a servant of God. Abraham being placed in the fire can refer to him being challenged by Satan. It re-emphasizes ALLAH'S promise, that Satan would not be able to destroy the prophets. Satan had to be cool and peaceful before Abraham. The Qur'an says, "*For over My servants no authority shalt thou have...*" (15:42).

According to the Qur'an, after ALLAH saved Abraham from the fire the leaders hatched another plan. "*Then they sought a*

strategy against him: but We made them the ones that lost most!"
(21:70).

It appears to me that whenever the enemies of man and truth are out voted or defeated at the table of justice, intelligence, and common sense, they always concoct another wicked plot. After Pharaoh saw that he could not outwit Moses, he tried to kill him. Pharaoh and his army chased Moses and his people across the desert. The Romans and the Jews tried to kill Jesus. History says the same of Prophet Muhammad. After the Prophet's (PBUH) message began defeating the false concepts and beliefs of the Arabs, the leadership felt threatened and stooped to such a low level as to plan his death. Of course they were unsuccessful.

Those of us who fight for the cause of truth and justice, those who seek to enlighten the masses and share the potent message of the Qur'an with the people, must always be aware of the fact that the enemies are always plotting and planning. However, there is no need to fear because ALLAH (GOD) has already given us excellent signs in history that He will protect the righteous believers. ALLAH also says, *"those before them did (also) devise plots; but in all things the master-planning is ALLAH'S (GOD'S). He knoweth the doings of every soul: and soon will the unbelievers know who gets home in the end."* (13:42).

CHAPTER 5

ABRAHAM GOES TO EGYPT

"And there was a famine in the land: And Abraham went down into Egypt to sojourn there; for the famine was grievous in the land."

The Scripture says Abraham went into Egypt. According to some of the reports going to Egypt meant receiving some of the benefits from Egypt. We also find that some of the Prophets came into Egypt as babies, or young in knowledge and experience. The Bible and Qur'an say this of Moses. The Scripture also says the same of Jesus (Bible, Matthew 2.13-15).

Joseph came into Egypt as a captive. Joseph was a slave who was sold to the Egyptians. Mythology says that one of the requirements for entering Egypt was to break or answer a riddle. In other words, you had to have some knowledge. If the reader will think about it, we are actually referring to three levels and three situations. A baby has very little knowledge or experience. Most people love babies. Adults control and form the baby's mind. Therefore, baby refers to an innocent and helpless state. Moses and Jesus were in an innocent and helpless state when they entered Egypt. It can be reasoned then that they were greatly influenced by the Egyptians. Joseph was not actually a baby, but he was a slave. This means he could at least think for himself to some extent and speak for himself. A slave or captive is one whose mobility is restricted. He has limited movement. Joseph could reason and speak for himself but he could not move about freely. If he wanted to leave Egypt, he could not because he was a captive. That situation symbolizes the thinking or planning stage. It alludes to the thought process and the initial idea. The mobility or movement represents the implementation of the idea or knowledge. Mobility represents freedom which symbolizes the knowledge in action. A good example of this is what the Qur'an says of Prophet Muhammad as a free man in the city: "*And thou art a freeman of this city....*" (90:2). It is also reported that Aisha said the Prophet Muhammad was the Qur'an living and walking.

The human being comes into the world just like Moses and Jesus came into Egypt--innocent and helpless. Egypt, like the world, will accept you if you come in as a baby, innocent. God asks man to come to him like that too. ALLAH (GOD) will reward and bless us for our humble posture, but the leaders of the world will take advantage of you. They will make you a mental slave. The next stage for man is like Joseph, to be able to think and speak for yourself. But until we get some resources of our own, we are enslaved to those who own the resources. We need resources in order to carry out a plan or idea. We say sometimes, "Brother, once I get some money, boy, I am going to put this idea to work." Egypt would accept those with good ideas and no resources. Egypt accepted slaves.

Egypt would accept those babies, slaves and men of knowledge. Abraham was a man of knowledge and intelligence. In other words he came into Egypt already prepared. He had already been taught by ALLAH (GOD), whereas Moses and Jesus learnt during and after their stay in Egypt. Abraham, unlike Joseph, had freedom. He was able to move about and leave. His stay was brief. These great men and Prophets are models and they point to certain developmental stages and processes in man. Abraham was not a baby or a slave when he entered Egypt. He was an enlightened, faithful human being. Abraham was like the adult who comes home and leaves when he wants to. Actually, what we see is the baby entering the home or society (Moses and Jesus). The young adult (Joseph) can think and speak but lives under the rule of his parents, therefore, he cannot come and go as he pleases. Finally you have the experienced and knowledgeable, independent adult, Abraham.

ABRAHAM BREAKS THE RIDDLE

If Abraham entered Egypt as a man, then he must have broken the riddle. He must have known the password. He must have had wisdom and knowledge. The proof that Abraham had the knowledge and was able to break the riddle, was the fact that he was able to out smart Pharaoh and get his wife Sarah back. The Bible says, *"And Pharaoh called Abram, and said, what is this that thou hast done unto me? Why didst thou not tell me that she was thy wife? What saidst thou, she is my sister? So I might have taken her to be my wife: now therefore behold thy wife, take her and go thy way.* " (Genesis 12:19).

Another indication that Abraham had the necessary knowledge to enter Egypt is the fact that he learned by looking at the stars, the moon and the sun. As I have already explained, there is a great deal of knowledge and usefulness that man obtains from the creation. When Abraham went to Egypt, he was a believer in the One God. In Egypt they believed in various gods. They had declined in their belief in the One God. Their major gods were Osiris, Isis and Horus. They were of the family of Ra the "supreme God".

In Egypt there were two main mystery systems of learning. They were called the Osirian mystery system and the Isisian mystery system. Osiris represented the sun and Isis represented the moon. The special people who were allowed into the Osirian system learned what was called the greater mysteries, because the sun is the greater light in the heavens. Therefore, Osiris, the sun, represented a certain knowledge for the special and chosen few. The Isisian mystery system taught the lesser mysteries. Those who were initiated in that school learned knowledge of the material aspect of life. The other systems and its students were symbolized by the star. Therefore, in Ancient Egypt, if a man said, "I have observed the setting of the stars, the moon and the sun and have arrived at the ultimate truth" it meant that he had seen the limits of the knowledge of each of those mystery systems, and had received greater wisdom and understanding. Even today, those who belong to esoteric secret societies use that same kind of language. For example, if a student of these systems says, "I know where the sun rises!" he is saying that he has received a certain degree of secret knowledge.

ALLAH blessed Abraham with the higher knowledge before he went to Egypt. He gained that knowledge through a natural process. So when he went to Egypt he already knew what to say and do in order to make progress. That is a great sign, that tells us that we don't need to join their secret fraternities and esoteric schools. They are nothing but slave camps. ALLAH demonstrated through Abraham that the sincere truth seeker will be rewarded with the supreme knowledge. Abraham was blessed with the science of creation and the true knowledge of ALLAH (GOD). The Egyptian had the high science of creation but they had lost the knowledge of the true God.

Egypt was also known as Mizraim which is a plural word, meaning Upper and Lower Egypt. This African country was the source of great knowledge and science. It was a highly advanced society. It is unlikely that Abraham did not learn anything from Egypt. In fact, in all probability he learned how to build from the Egyptians. The Egyptians were master builders. They were well versed in geometry, physics, et cetera. Abraham built a house which is called the Kab'ah. The Ancient Egyptians had two words which alluded to the spiritual or the soul. They are called Ka and Ba. I will discuss these two concepts in a subsequent chapter. Ancient Egypt was divided into two kingdoms: Upper Egypt and Lower, Egypt. Upper Egypt focused on the spiritual. The King or Pharaohs of Upper Egypt wore a symbol of a hawk on his crown, which alluded to the higher or spiritual concerns. The King of Lower Egypt wore a symbol of a snake on his crown representing material and rational wisdom. These two kingdoms were later united by an African king named Menes. He wore a double crown with a symbol of the hawk and the snake. Because a bird flies in the sky, which is above the earth, it has been identified with the spiritual. The snake is confined to the earth, therefore it symbolizes the lower or earthly material plane. The double crown represented the union of the material and the spiritual, the heaven and the earth.

33

SHU

As I have mentioned, Ancient Egypt had many myths and concepts about God. There was an Egyptian god named "Shu". It is said that he was arched between the sky and the earth, somewhat like the shoes that we wear today. Actually, the word shoe refers to the ancient god Shu. The story of the mythological god says that he separated the heaven-god, "Nut", from the earth-god, "Geb". Shu is called the "god of air". According to the book The Gods and Symbols of Ancient Egypt, "...the Ancient Egyptians myths were the doings of the gods at the beginning of the world, but these events were symbols expressing the present organization of things. The god of air, Shu, separates heaven (Nut) and earth (Geb), a symbolic act denoting a consciousness of up and down, light and darkness, good and evil." (page 8).

THOTH

There was another important Egyptian God by the name "Thoth". According to to the myth, he sprung from the head of another god named Seth. Thoth was called the "Lord of time and Reckoner of years." It is also said that Thoth was the inventor of writing. The word "thought" is derived from the mythological figure Thoth. Thinking is associated with the head and writing is an expression of thinking.

Although Egypt had a pantheon of gods, it was still a highly advanced and enlightened country. Much of today's knowledge can be traced back to Ancient Egypt. The pyramids are an indication of the high level of sophisticated knowledge that the Africans of Egypt possessed. In fact the pyramids represent Egypt and its sciences. In order to enter Egypt or the pyramids you had to come by way of the Sphinx, which sat as a guard looking east at the rising of the sun. As I pointed out in my book, Freemasonry, Ancient Egypt and the Islamic Destiny the Sphinx presented a riddle of which the answer was man. The Sphinx is a huge structure, the form of which consists of a man's face, an eagle, a bull and a lion. The Sphinx symbolizes man rising above and controlling his animal nature. Professor Hilton Hotema explains "... Again the Sphinx symbolizes the Microcosmic with the Mind and Spirit of the human rising up out of the animal desires and passions. It is the riddle of the ages and man is the answer." The Mysterious Sphinx (page 36). Legend has it that anyone who failed to answer the riddle correctly was killed and consumed by the Sphinx.

Abraham mastered his lower passions and animal nature. The Bible and Qur'an say he was willing to sacrifice his son which was a physical part of him. It also says that he sacrificed a ram. The human being should not be killed and used as a sacrifice because the human being is really a mind, an intellect and a spirit. Animals are to be sacrificed for human survival. Abraham sacrificing the ram represents several things, one of which is his great discipline and control over selfish desires. Imam W. D. Muhammad explained, "This sacrifice symbolically indicates that we, as individuals, are first responsible for ourselves. The shedding of blood symbolizes our victory over the life drive of the animal nature within us. We are not to be controlled by our animal instincts, desires and appetites. We should rise to a higher level. We should discipline the life drives of our animal inclinations to yield obedience to ALLAH" (Prayer and Al-Islam p. 155).

THE DOOR

The temples in Ancient Egypt had very huge doors. There were several reasons for this. Some say it is because the Africans were very tall and big people. In some cases that is true; however, there were more profound reasons for this. The huge structures, monuments, et cetera, represent a psychology and a fear tactic. They were intended to overwhelm the individual. The temple was a place of learning, instructions and initiation. The huge doors represent the large volume of knowledge that one could receive if he was allowed to enter and learn. The Sphinx not only represented a guard at the gate, but it was actually a door or entrance way into the pyramids or Egypt. Professor Hotema writes"...Beneath the breast of the Sphinx was the secret door to the underground passage, well guarded and opening by the application of a secret device, known only to a few select person" (The Mysterious Sphinx p. 35).

A door is an opening. It represents the act of giving and receiving. For example, some doors are pushed open, which indicates giving. If we think about it, when we enter a room by pushing the door open, our arm extends outward as if giving something. Upon leaving the room, we may pull the door open which brings our arms inward to our body. In some cases it is the reverse. Sometimes we enter by pulling the door open and we exit by pushing it out. If the reader tries this he would see that it is true. The opening of the door represents the natural and dual process of giving and receiving, or learning and teaching. Those who enter by pushing the door open, already have something to give, therefore, they extend a helping hand first. As a result they may receive a good reward.

Sometimes it is just as difficult to leave a place as it is to enter. Leaving Egypt also required a certain knowledge. The Scripture says that Pharaoh did not want Moses and his people to leave. He wanted to keep them in bondage. Abraham was blessed by ALLAH (GOD) with universal knowledge. He knew how to enter and exit. According to the Bible and Qur'an, he entered by pushing the door open, by extending his hand. Abraham gave something. The Scriptures say he gave Pharaoh his wife, which just means he gave of himself and his responsibility. A man has a responsibility to his wife. God gives him the responsibility of maintaining and protecting her. The Scripture says Abraham did not want to give the King his wife, so he told him that Sarah was his sister. It is reported that the King would take the wife and kill the husband. The Bible says Abraham said, "Therefore it shall come to pass, when the Egyptians shall see thee, that they shall say this is his wife: and they will kill me, but they will save thee alive. Say, I pray thee, thou art my sister, that it may be well with me for thy sake; and my soul shall live because of thee" (Genesis 12:12,13).

ABRAHAM LEAVES EGYPT

Abraham was a free thinking man. His mind was not limited or restricted to the immediate environment. Abraham left Egypt with more than what he had when he went there. He received his wife back, he received his material resources back. In addition to that he was able to bring his nephew Lot or Lut out of Egypt with him. The Bible says, "And Abram went up out of Egypt he and his wife, and all that he had and Lot with him, into the south. And Abram was very rich in cattle, in silver and in gold." (Genesis 13:1,2). See the book Freemasonry, Ancient Egypt and the Islamic Destiny for symbols and meaning of silver and gold. According to some accounts the King gave to Abraham the Egyptian woman named Hagar. Haykal reports, "He (The King) returned her (Sarah) to Ibrahim (Abraham) blamed him for the lie, and gave him a number of gifts, one of which was a slave girl by the name of Hagar." (The Life of Muhammad p.24).

Abraham left Egypt with an additional responsibility. His knowledge and freedom required responsibility. He had to be responsible for the well being of Hagar. This tells us then that freedom requires responsibility and that a free man without responsibility is actually immature and unrefined. The Bible says, "to whom much is given, much is required." To be mentally free in this world today is a blessing. We must learn how to leave an oppressive environment. There is a great lesson in Abraham leaving Egypt. We should learn what we can that is good and beneficial, and then make a mental moral and spiritual exodus. Abraham represents the rational and emotional urge in man that seeks expression in the open environment. ALLAH says in the Holy Qur'an, "O My servants who believe! Truly spacious is my earth: Therefore serve ye Me (and Me alone)!" (29:56).

37

CHAPTER 6

ABRAHAM AND MELCHIZEDEK

According to the Bible, after Abraham came out of Egypt, he met a very mysterious man named Melchizedek. "...And Melchizedek king of Salem brought forth bread and wine and he was the priest of the most high God. And he blessed him, and said Blessed be Abram of the most high God, possessor of heaven and earth." (Genesis 14:18,19). The bread and wine symbolizes material and spiritual knowledge. Bread is heavy, it increases the body weight, therefore it is related to the physical. Wine is symbolic of spiritual activity because it excites the senses. In fact, today wine is called "spirits". Abraham received some knowledge from Melchizedek.

It is also reported, however, that Melchizedek was very mysterious and that he was "Without father, without mother, without descent, having neither beginning of days, nor end of life...." (Hebrews 7:3).

He is also referred to as the "King of peace and righteousness". Abraham did not receive spiritual and material knowledge from Melchizedek and just turn and walk away. Abraham gave something back. The Bible says he gave Melchizedek "the tenth of the spoils."

Christian Theologians, Priests, Bible Scholars and students of esoteric wisdom have pondered over the question "Who was Melchizedek?" Some say he was God; others say he was Jesus. The Bible says, "....even Jesus, made an high priest for even after the order of Melchisedec." (Hebrew 6:20).

Actually Melchizedek represents an eternal principle that was created in man. It is the tendency and desire to be righteous and peaceful. Melchizedek represents the good nature of man that was placed in Adam from the very beginning. Both the Bible and Qur'an tell us that Adam was created without father, mother or descent. The Qur'an says ALLAH created man in the best mold and that all the sons of Adam have dignity. (H. Q. 95:4). Not only does Melchizedek represent righteousness and perfection, but he also alludes to God's eternal law of compensation. Whatever we do we will be held accountable for it. If we give righteousness then on the day of judgement we will receive our just due. It is just like working on a job or providing a service. You give your labor you get paid. Melchizedek represents that give and take process. It is natural. An excellent example is the fact that we inhale oxygen from the plants and trees so that we can live, and we exhale carbon monoxide which the plants inhale.

Melchizedek gave Abraham bread (material knowledge) and wine (spiritual instructions); and Abraham gave him a tenth of the spoils. The tenth represents "conscious awareness". It means Abraham gave him his attention. Abraham was alert, he understood what Melchizedek was expressing when he gave him the gifts. Even today ten refers to conscious awareness, alertness. After a fighter has been knocked down to the canvas he has to be up by the count of ten. If he is not up by the count of ten, it means he is knocked out, un-conscious, un-alert. The tenth day of the Hajj is very important for the Muslim. It is the tenth of Dhu-Al-Hijjah that marks the beginning of the Feast of Sacrifice. Hammudah Abdalati writes, "It falls on the tenth day of Dhu-L-Hijjah, the last month of the Muslim year, following completion of the course of Hajj (pilgrimage to Makkah), an extremely devotional course." (Islam in Focus p. 72). Ten represents "conscious sacrifice", therefore Abraham giving Melchizedek a tenth of the spoils suggests that Abraham made a conscious sacrifice to righteousness and peace.

The act of sacrificing does not help or enrich ALLAH (GOD), rather it purifies our heart and soul. Actually, Abraham did something to improve his worth before ALLAH (GOD). He made a conscious sacrifice not a blind sacrifice. If we are blind or ignorant we may sacrifice the wrong thing. We may think it is the object (animal, money, time) that reaches ALLAH (GOD). The conscious person knows it is his sincerity that reaches ALLAH. The Qur'an says "It is not their meat nor their blood, that reaches ALLAH: it is your piety that reaches Him." (22:37) - ALLAH-U-AKBAR

CHAPTER 7

ABRAHAM, SARAH AND HAGAR

Abraham was married to Sarah for several years before he married Hagar, who was from Egypt. Sarah was unable to bare children for many years. It is reported that she agreed to Abraham marrying Hagar and having a child. Shortly, after their marriage Hagar bore Abraham a son, Isma'il. Abraham devoted a lot of time and attention to his son and his African wife, Hagar. Consequently, Sarah felt neglected, became jealous and requested that Hagar and Isma'il be cast out. Abraham being the intelligent man that he was, took heed and separated Hagar from Sarah. I am sure Abraham tried his best to please the both of them, and treated them justly. However, the Qur'an tells us that *"Ye are never able to be fair and just as between women, even if it is your ardent desire...." But if they disagree (and must part), ALLAH will provide abundance for all from His All-reaching bounty: For ALLAH is He that careth for all and is Wise."* (4:129-130).

History tells us that the Prophet Muhammad's wives became jealous also and he had to move one of them to another place. In the book the Life of Muhammad by Muhammad Husayn Haykal, the wives of the Prophet became jealous of Maryam the mother of his son Ibrahim. Haykal writes "Every day Muhammad would visit the house of Maryam in order to take another look at his son's radiant face and to reassure himself of the newborn's continued health and growth. All this incited the strongest jealousy among the barren wives." (page 433).

Concerning Sarah and Hagar's disagreement, some report that it was based on an incident that occurred between Isaac and Isma'il. Hagar is referred to as a slave-girl. According to some claims, Sarah felt that she and her child Isaac were better than Hagar and Isma'il because she (Sarah) was never a slave. Although she had a difficult time giving birth ALLAH did

41

eventually bless her with a child - Isaac. The Qur'an states, "*And his wife was standing (there) and she laughed: But We gave her glad tidings of Isaac, and after him of Jacob. She said "Alas for me! Shall I bear a child, seeing I am an old women, and my husband here is an old man? That would indeed be a wonderful thing!*" (11:71,72). In that same sura ALLAH reminds us of Abraham's character. "*For Abraham was without doubt, forbearing (of faults), compassionate, and given to look to ALLAH.*" (11:75)

HAGAR AND ISMAIL IN THE DESERT

According to the story, Abraham realizing that the two women could not live in the same household peacefully decided to take Hagar and their son Isma'il out to the valley of Makkah. He left them with food and water.

This event is extremely important not only because of its historic value, but also its moral implications. Would a man of such noble character, wisdom and faith cast his wife and an infant out into the desert? Abraham is considered a friend of God, a man of intelligence and a model of excellence. To say that Abraham cast Hagar and Isma'il out into the wilderness simply because the two women could not get along, appears to me to be a defamation of Abraham's character. It also has racial overtones. The Bible says Sarah was fair, which suggests that she was of light complexion. It is a historical fact that Hagar was a black African women. It appears as though the African people were rejected and cast out by a righteous servant of God. It is extremely important that we think for ourselves and don't always rely on other people's reports as the only source of information.

Abraham casting Hagar and Isma'il out into the desert has great spiritual meaning and significance. Those who study this story will see that it shows the progression of life. It reveals the growth and development of man. Hagar was rejected, but through her came the last Messenger, Prophet Muhammad, the model human being. He is a descendent of Hagar and Isma'il. The Bible says, "that which was last shall be first and the keystone that the builders rejected will become the headstone." The Qur'an says ALLAH rotates the rule.

HAGAR SEARCHES FOR WATER

After the provisions had run out, Hagar went looking for food and water. She became desperate and ran to and fro seven times between two hills, Safa and Marwah, seeking water. It is said, that while she was seeking water she left Isma'il alone. When she returned she discovered water coming forth from under the baby, Ismail's heel. There she discovered a well, which today is called the well of Zam Zam.

So important was this event that during hajj Muslims are required to repeat the act of running back and forth seven times between Safa and Marwah in remembrance and respect of Hagar, the black African women from Egypt. I emphasize the fact that she was an African women only because there are those who argue that so-called Black people have no legitimate place in the history of Islam and world events. There are those who claim that people of color have not contributed anything to the world. There are racist people who feel that Africans and their descendents cannot and should not think for themselves because we are incapable of thinking and acting intelligent.

Some people would have the world believe that the religion of Al-Islam enslaved the Black man of Africa. Therefore, in defence of Al-Islam, it is important to show that the African as well as the Arab was among the first to establish the religion. The first house ever built for the glorification of ALLAH (GOD) was built by Abraham and Isma'il, the son of a Black Egyptian women. Therefore, if we trace the origin of the religion back to our father Abraham, we will find that the black African was there to help lay the first corner stone.

CHAPTER 8

HAGAR IN THE DESERT: A MODERN REALITY

According to some reports our ancestor, Hagar, was once a slave. She also was cast into the desert or wilderness. History tells us that before the Europeans came into Africa and destroyed its civilization, some of us were slaves there. Some of us were servants of the King. Some of the Africans were captives of war. Hagar was an Egyptian women and she was the slave of an Egyptian King. We must understand, however, that slavery in Africa was altogether different from the kind of slavery that was established by the Europeans. The level of cruelty, dependence, and inhuman treatment that accompanied the European Caucasian slave system was the worst in the annals of history.

Some African Americans, just like Hagar, were once enslaved by their own people. It is also reported that Hagar was cast out into the desert or wilderness because of jealousy. Sarah became jealous of Hagar because Abraham was paying attention to Hagar and the baby. As I mentioned, Sarah felt that she was better than Hagar and that she (Hagar) was not worthy of such good treatment, therefore, she insisted that Hagar be cast out.

History also tells us that the African American people were cast out into the desert and wilderness of European racism and slavery because of jealousy and white supremacy. When the White man came into Africa and saw the great achievements that we had made as a people, the flames of hatred and jealousy began to burn like a raging fire. When that White man from the caves and mountains of Europe saw our ancestors living on a highly advanced scientific level, when he saw the beautiful climate, physical environment that ALLAH (GOD) had blessed us with, when he saw that God was giving us attention, he became angry and vicious. The Caucasians lived like savages in Europe at the time when Blacks were living like dignified human beings. This is a fact. The White man was in the dark. Europeans were raising cannibals while the Africans were raising great men like Hannibal.

God had blessed the Africans with fertile land, clean air, wisdom, social unity and respect. The Africans had a high regard for family and a deep respect and love for the elders. When the White man of Europe travelled from West to East and saw the splendid light of civilization, his dark mind and heart grew jealous and hard. The Black Africans were/are very spiritual, whereas the Europeans are extremely physical.

The White man's hatred and jealousy caused him to despise us and enslave us. He cast us into a barren land. Symbolically speaking, women represent society which produces cultural habits. We are a product of our society. Therefore, Sarah represented a society that became jealous of another society.

The African American, like Hagar, has been searching for water in the wilderness and desert of America . Water represents life, it is essential for the survival of life. Not only does water sustain life but it is the birth place of life. The Holy Qur'an states "It is He who has created man from water." (25:54). Also see 21:30.

Hagar ran to and fro between two hills Safa and Marwah seven times seeking that which would sustain her and her baby's life. She was searching for that from which life begins. She ran seven times, which means she made a complete search. Seven represents completion. Remember she was from Egypt, a place of great symbolisms. As we mentioned, in Egypt there was the mythological figure called Isis, symbolized by the moon. Isis had seven veils. She represented complete secrecy. The moon comes out at night. Darkness or night covers the day, therefore it also alludes to secrecy. To keep something in the dark means to keep it hidden. The Holy Qur'an says, *"By the Night as it conceals (the light)."* (92:1).

45

Hagar running between Safa and Mawah seven times may mean that she was applying the symbolism of Ancient Egypt, and that she was trying to uncover the veils or secrets of the desert in hopes of finding water (life). The reports of this story say she was unsuccessful. Remember she was a slave in Egypt which means she did not know how to enter Egypt, she did not know how to break the riddle of Isis and unlock the secrets. She was kept out of the knowledge. But she tried. She ran desperately to and fro. She was driven by her spirit, her natural instinct and her love for her baby. God blessed her. The story says when she returned to her baby she found the water (life) that she was looking for. In other words, when she (society) returned to its original nature and posture before God, her life was sustained. The Bible says, "unless you come as babies you cannot enter paradise."

Water is the birthplace or beginning of life. A baby is the beginning of human life in terms of our exposure to the outer environment. Therefore, baby and water go together. Water is also symbolic of moral life and natural revelation. Another example of water and baby being together is Moses being placed in the water. We see that Isma'il and Moses are associated with water because both of them, as babies, were associated with water.

Returning to Hagar, the story says that when Hagar came back to Isma'il she found the water (life) she needed. Some accounts of this story say the baby laid on the ground and as he moved his heel several times, he uncovered some water; then Hagar came and found the water under the baby's heel.

THE HEEL

The heel is a round bone and it represents spiritual activity and spiritual balance. Isma'il moved his heel several times upon the earth. Movement represents activity. As I explained in my other two books, Freemasonry Ancient Egypt and The Islamic Destiny and Al-Islam, Christianity and Freemasonry, a circle represents the spiritual, and the square represents the material. All things that are round or circular are capable of moving. Round objects can roll. The heel as a round bone represents spiritual, and the movement of the heel symbolizes the life or activity of that spirit.

The baby rubbing his heel on the material earth symbolizes the act of applying spiritual activity to material life. In other words, if we keep spiritual conscious or spiritual activity in our material life, and in the society, then the moral (water) substance will continue to flow in the society. Morality is the foundation of civilized society. The heel is a part of the foot which is our foundation. We stand upon our feet, they support us. The water coming from under Ismail's feet means the moral life must be at the foundation, not up in the mountains. The leadership that stands above the masses keeps a code of ethics and morality among themselves, but they don't give it to the masses. In secret, the leadership practices very high moral wisdom and principles. They use the high moral codes of the Qur'an among themselves, but they encourage the masses to be immoral and indecent. If you don't belong to their secret order, they won't give you the moral sustenance that you need for your life. Hagar represents the deprived masses who go to the government seeking life. She represents the rejected and despised.

In Egyptian Mythology it is said that Isis searched diligently to restore her husband's life. Hagar, our ancestor, also searched constantly and persistently for the means to sustain her baby's life, but she went to the wrong place. African-Americans have also been going to the wrong places pleading and begging for food and water. We have gone to the Republican party's Mountains and The Democratic party's Mountains looking for water. Some of us have gone between the mountains seven times; some of us are completely in love with the White establishment. Some of our leaders are so in love with the Democratic party and the White establishment until they will do anything to be accepted by their White slave master. The brother is too proud or too ignorant to see and realize that the answer is within himself and his people. The brother is too ignorant to return to his own people. Some of our Black leaders act as if they are bound to these two Mountains (Democratic and Republican) by some kind of "Cable tow."

47

Most of the Black leaders are Christian Reverends and Masons. They read the Bible and see what it says about Hagar not being able to find water outside of herself and her baby, but yet they go far away from the moral foundation of themselves and their people seeking water from the White man, who has proven beyond a shadow of a doubt that he does not intend to share the throne of leadership with a shoe-shinning, tap-dancing, slave-minded, begging Blackman. The answer to our survival and progress is at the feet of our youth who are the foundation of our future.

African Americans have been looking to the Democratic Mountains and the Republican Mountains for life too long. Running between two hills or mountains also alludes to the church and the Government. The Western Church and the Government have not provided us with what we need. The proof of this is that most of our leaders are Christian Reverends but do not demonstrate a real fear of God. They don't tell us that if we don't vote, or decide to have God's truth in our life, that we will be in a bad situation. They don't tell us that. They say, "If you don't vote for the *Democratic party* the Republicans will get in and you will have hell in your life, and we will be in a bad situation."

The answer is within. ALLAH (GOD) has blessed us with a good human spirit, an excellent nature, and a mind that is as potent and sophisticated as any other human being on the face of this earth. All we have to do is humble ourselves before God, apply the spiritual activity of Scripture to our material appetite, and stand upon moral principles. The Bible says the Kingdom of God is within. The Scriptures tell us that God blessed Abraham and Hagar with a son, Isma'il, who became a Prophet of God. An even greater blessing came with the birth of Prophet Muhammad (PBUH) in that God rewarded Abraham, Hagar and Isma'il by choosing one of their descendents as the Model and most excellent human being to ever walk the planet earth. ALLAH chose a descendent from a slave woman to be the best of all the creation and the last messenger and Prophet of ALLAH (GOD). Isma'il received the revelation from below his feet, and Prophet

48

Muhammad Ibn Abdullah (PBUH) received the Last Revelation, the Qur'an from above.

If the African American will turn to the Holy Qur'an, or good, sound, virtuous, principles---return to God, and hold on to sacred, moral principles, and work hard, we will become leaders over ourselves and others. Our family life will be restored; we will achieve economic dignity, political dignity, social unity and above all human excellence.

CHAPTER 9

ABRAHAM'S SACRIFICE

"Then, when (the son) reached (the age of serious) work with him, He said: 'O my son! I see in a vision That I offer thee in sacrifice: Now see what is thy view. (The son) said: 'O my father! Do as thou art commanded: Thou will find me, if ALLAH so wills, one practicing patience and constancy!" *(H. Q. 37:102)*

Abraham was not only a rational, intelligent and logical person, but he was also a man of deep devotion, sincere faith and obedience to ALLAH (GOD). ALLAH had blessed Abraham with so much knowledge and wisdom until his (Abraham's) faith became so enriched and genuine that he was willing to kill, or sacrifice, his own flesh and blood son for the pleasure of ALLAH (GOD). It was this act of devotion and willingness on the part of Abraham that led ALLAH to make Abraham the Imam, leader or father of all the nations. Imam W. D. Muhammad stated, "Abraham is called the man of faith by the Jews, the Christians and then by the Muslims. He was no fool; he was a very wise man. He didn't follow faith in any spooky way. His intelligence led him to faith." (Muslim Journal 8/14/88). A. A. Maududi, in explaining the importance of intelligence and faith, writes: "The Arabic word "Iman" which we have translated into English as faith literally means 'to know; to believe, and to be convinced beyond a shadow of a doubt!' Thus, *faith is firm belief arising out of knowledge and conviction."* (Towards Understanding Islam p.18).

Abraham was originally called Abram, which means father or leader. His willingness to obey ALLAH (GOD) earned him the title of Abraham, father of the nations. According to the Qur'an both Abraham and his son were willing to carry out the sacrifice. This tells us then, that just as Abraham was willing to kill his son for the pleasure of ALLAH, Isma'il was also willing to die for the pleasure of ALLAH. Think about this! An older man ready to kill his son, and a young boy willing to accept death. Some people are willing to kill for a cause but not die for it, while others are willing to die for a cause but not kill for it. Still others are willing to do both. Abraham was willing to do both. As we mentioned in a previous chapter, Abraham accepted to be put into the fire for his belief and actions.

In another sense we can also understand this willingness on the part of Abraham and his son as representing certain qualities in Abraham. The son is a biological and genetic extension of the parents. Therefore, the son's patience and constancy was a reflection of what was in Abraham. ALLAH did not want him (Abraham) to kill this.

ALLAH says in the Qur'an, *"So when they had both submitted their wills (to ALLAH), and he had laid him prostrate on his forehead (for sacrifice), We called out to him, "O Abraham! Thou hast already fulfilled the vision!" Thus indeed do We reward those who do right."* (37:103-105). ALLAH commanded Abraham to kill and sacrifice a sheep (ram) instead of his son. This was a great test for Abraham. The Qur'an says, *"For this was obviously a trial."* (37:106)

To sacrifice basically means to "give of something that you own which is of some value and use to you". As already stated, this story shows us how sincere Abraham was and how sincere and faithful we who call ourselves Muslims and believers should be. There are very important principles promulgated in the idea of sacrifice.

ALLAH stopped Abraham from sacrificing his son. To kill his son would not only have given man the wrong idea of worship and sacrifice, but it would have stopped his son who was destined to become a prophet and a co-builder of the Kab'ah. ALLAH blessed Isma'il and Isaac with the noble title and responsibility of

Prophet. The Qur'an states, "*Also mention in the Book (The story of) Isma'il: He was (strictly) true to what he promised, and he was an apostle (and) a prophet.*" (19:54). The Qur'an also says, "*And We gave him the good news of Isaac, a prophet, one of the Righteous.*" (37:113).

It appears for all practical purposes that ALLAH never allows any man to kill or stop his prophets or messengers. ALLAH said he would protect his servants. Muslims don't believe that the Prophets of ALLAH (GOD) were killed. We don't believe that Jesus was a sacrificial lamb who was slaughtered by his enemies. ALLAH blessed Jesus and the other prophets to live a full life. If Abraham would have killed his son, the foolish men or women could point to that as a justification for killing their children.

Our children have some of our traits. To kill one of them is to kill that trait in them. The Qur'an says Abraham's son was patient and steadfast. We can understand this to mean that Abraham was also patient and steadfast, and that ALLAH did not want him to kill that nature, but to keep it and preserve it. Use that patient and steadfast nature, along with the rational intellectual abilities and faith, to help build the Kaaba. Human beings cannot sacrifice patience or constancy. Those are individual qualities. We cannot make other people patient. We can teach them the importance of patience and perseverance, but we cannot give it to them. So to sacrifice those qualities is to destroy them in yourself. ALLAH did not want Abraham to do that. ALLAH wanted Abraham to sacrifice something that he could give to the people. Abraham sacrificed a ram.

The ram is the male, or leader, among the sheep. Sheep are clickish and passive. Sheep are easily domesticated. They are also a good source of clothing. They, like other animals, have a strong social conscience. They are peaceful and humble. Some of them dwell in mountains while others dwell in low places. Sheep are useful to man. We get wool from the sheep. Wool is used mostly during the winter. We wear wool clothing when it is cold outside. Wool keeps us warm. The Sheep's skin is also worn by man.

"There is not an animal (that lives) on earth, Nor a being that flies on its wings, but (forms part of) communities like you." (6:38)

THE RAM: SECRET PASSIVE LEADERSHIP

The Ram is the leader of a passive humble animal. ALLAH told Abraham to sacrifice or kill the leader among the sheep. Man is not supposed to become so weak and pious until he withdraws from the world. We are not supposed to allow others to lead us to slaughter without putting up a fight. Our leaders should not be weak and extremely peaceful meek sheep. The sheep represents a certain characteristic in man. It alludes to that tendency to become withdrawn from the challenges of life and society and only concern ourselves with those in our group. ALLAH wants us to share our social conscience with the people of the world. The love and respect that we give to our immediate relatives should be shared with the community at large. Abraham expanded his social activities. He sacrificed that tendency and fed it to all the people. That is why he became known as the "father or leader of all the nations". The ram is only the leader of one nation. Abraham was the leader of just one nation until he graduated to the level of Imam or leader of the multitudes.

Many of our leaders today belong to the sheepish order of secrecy and esoteric wisdom. They only allow the wisdom to be shared with those in their secret order. Many of our leaders have received "Lambskin aprons" from their "Worshipful masters" as a token of their innocence. They are told that it is a badge of a mason and a symbol of innocence. A badge is a means of identification. Therefore, if a man wears a sheepskin apron then he must be a part of a sheepish order. Which means he possesses a certain kind of knowledge and quality. Imam W. D. Muhammad explained, "God told him (Abraham) to sacrifice the sheep and feed it to the needy and the poor. "What is sacrifice?" he asked. It means that you have done away with that order. The sheepish order is an order that keeps its wisdom in the ram; and its wisdom governs the order of the sheep, but through the ram. The sheep can not have that wisdom, it is only for the ram. It is only for the male, the leader in the sheepish community." (Lecture: A Discipline for Achieving Man's Inherent Worth).

Muslims make the sacrifice during the tenth day of Hajj. As I have explained, ten represents conscious awareness or alertness. This means we should make a conscious sacrifice of the animal drives and selfish tendency in us. How do we kill the secret societies? We kill them by making the people conscious and aware of what they know and do. We expose them to the world by sharing the knowledge that they keep hidden in their secret vaults, with the larger community. This will free them and us. Many of those who are apart of the leadership of the sheep really want to be free. They are tired of being hunted by wild, furious wolves and wild beast. I know for a fact that some of the African Americans who belong to the secret orders, want to share the knowledge with the people, but they can't because they have taken a death oath.

WOOL

Wool represents that which helps maintain and preserve the social affections in man. We wear wool during the cold months. Cold represents apathy, selfishness, lack of affections. When we say a person is "cold hearted" we mean he does not care. Cold is associated with death. During the winter the trees and plant life dies. The human being covers himself in wool to keep warm. A warm hearted person is a caring and considerate person. Wool, then symbolizes social knowledge and concerns. We wear wool coats, pants, sweaters et cetera to maintain our body temperature. If our body temperature drops too low we may die. Wool also alludes to that knowledge which covers us and protects us from the social death. This secret knowledge should be shared with the people. Abraham shared the knowledge with the people.

Let us not be weak sheep. Let us not be selfish and fearful. Some of our leaders that are apart of the sheepish or secret orders are afraid to break from their masters. Some of them are like those sheep that prefer to stay on the Democratic party's mountain . We should not be afraid to come down from the political mountains that this world has made for us. We need to sacrifice that tendency to live in the mountains forever. The Democratic party and the Republican party also identify themselves by animals.

CHAPTER 10

THE DONKEY AND THE ELEPHANT

ALLAH tells us that he has given us signs in animals, man, mountains, et cetera. ALLAH wants us to look at the creation and gain wisdom. In our modern times in America there are two major political parties which stand firm like mountains. One represents the right, and the other represents the left. One represents the social labor force, and the other represents the rational intelligence. The Democratic party is symbolized by the "Donkey", and the Republican party by the "Elephant". Although they are two parties, they are supposed to have one purpose. That is the fulfillment of the American dream and destiny. ALLAH has given man two eyes but one vision, two ears but we hear one sound. We should understand that this country, America, has taken much from the Holy Qur'an and the Sunnah of Muhammad. As I have mentioned in previous writings, those who established this America and its political system were Freemasons. Many of the principles and concepts of the Holy Qur'an are intertwined into the American system.

We are not animals. We are not elephants or donkeys. However, some people exemplify the characteristics of these animals. This world thinks that African Americans and the common people are dumb jackasses. A donkey is a stupid, unreliable work animal. The sound of his voice is painful to the ears. His ears are big but he acts like he cannot hear any words of wisdom. Therefore, a dumb, ignorant person is said to be like a donkey with a bunch of books on his back. The Qur'an says the similitude of those who were charged with the (obligation of the Mosaic Law) but who subsequently failed in those (obligations), is that of a donkey which carries huge tomes (But understands them not) (62:5). The Democratic party is a party of donkeys. That is why the manipulators tricked us into changing from the Republican party (The Elephant) to the Democratic party (The Donkey). We should tell the world that the party is over for us; we are not playing any more animal games; we belong to the peoples' destiny or the human progress movement. The donkey is a small animal and the elephant is a big animal.

The Elephant, unlike the donkey, is very intelligent. He has an excellent memory. The Elephant adapts to different situations very well. The Elephant represents intelligence. Because he is so huge he represents material intelligence. The Republicans are known as the materially wealthy party. They are considered the rich class. They pride themselves on their past record. They remember to tell us that it was a Republican who freed the slaves.

Comparatively speaking, the elephant is a better symbol than the donkey. History tells us of a great Black man named Hannibal who crossed the Alps with elephants. Prophet Muhammad was born during the "Year of the Elephant". The Bible tells us of a donkey that saw an angel with a flaming sword and began to talk back to his master. The Bible says the donkey said, "Why has thou hit me these three times?" (Numbers 22:22-32). The Bible also speaks of a donkey that was tied and Jesus told his disciples to untie the donkey and bring it to him. Jesus rode into the city on a donkey.

The Elephant has a trunk and it sounds like a trumpet. The Bible and Qur'an say that on the day of Judgement a trumpet will be blown. The Qur'an says the sinners will sound like donkeys whose voice is the worst of the animals.

CHAPTER 11

ABRAHAM AND ISMAIL: TWO MASTER BUILDERS

"And remember Abraham and Isma'il raised the foundations of the House (with this prayer): "Our Lord! Accept (this service) from us: For thou Art the All-Hearing, The All-Knowing. Our Lord! Make us Muslims, bowing to Thy (will), and our progeny a people Muslim, bowing to Thy (will), And show us our places for the celebration of (due) rites; And turn unto us (in Mercy): For Thou Art the Oft-Returning, Most Merciful..."
(2:127,128)

Abraham and his son Isma'il built the first house for the worship of ALLAH (GOD). The Qur'an says that as they laid the foundation they asked God to accept their service or work. They asked ALLAH to make them Muslims bowing to His Will. They laid the foundation of the Kaaba on faith, sincerity and respect for ALLAH (GOD). The Kaaba was built on "Taqwah" (God consciousness). Abraham and Isma'il actually built a physical structure that still stands today in the Holy City of Mekkah. This means that they did not just have faith, but they had knowledge. It takes knowledge to build a structure. All physical structures or objects are themselves a source of knowledge. Any building that we see contains knowledge. For example, some people can look at an automobile and see right away how to reproduce or make an automobile. A builder sees the knowledge in a building quicker than a person who is not a builder. For example those people who helped to build the Empire State Building in New York, when they see that building, they see work, they see difficulty, they see geometry, physics, masonry, chemistry, et cetera. When I see that building, I see just another tall building. Those who have knowledge see great wisdom, precision and accuracy.

Abraham and Isma'il apparently knew how to use the square, the plumb, and the level. Obviously ALLAH'S (GOD'S) two prophets knew how to use the tools of construction. Although the Kaaba is a simple structure, it contains a vast body of ancient wisdom and spiritual value. The Kaaba preserves the knowledge that was used by Abraham and Isma'il when they built it. Imam W. D. Muhammad, in explaining the importance of protecting knowledge, pointed out that one of the ways to do this is through construction. He said you protect it by building (Imam W. D. Muhammad Speaks from Harlem Part 2). Abraham and Isma'il were Master Builders who preserved the great knowledge of the unification and oneness of humanity. ALLAH (GOD) blessed them to live and overcome all obstacles. They were not slain by Jubela, Jubelo and Jubelum. They were not killed by any trinitarian conspiracy. In fact, the three major religions Christianity, Islam and Judaism believe that Abraham is the father of their faith and have the greatest respect and admiration for him.

Abraham connects many of the essential aspects of human life. He was a man of knowledge, faith, obedience and charity. He did not only learn and teach, he utilized and protected the knowledge so that we today can benefit from studying the Kaaba.

A LIGHT FROM HEAVEN

According to some reports, Abraham was given a sign by ALLAH (GOD) as to where to build the Kaaba. It is said that a star or meteorite fell from the sky and Abraham, upon seeing this, concluded that it was a sign from ALLAH. This star was white and glowing with light before it fell to the earth. As it came through the earth's atmosphere it burned and became black. some say this black stone was used as the corner stone for the Kaaba. If we think about it, we will see that actually there was a connection between the heavens and the earth, or the spiritual and the material. Our destiny is not in the sky of extreme spiritualism, but in the earth of reality. The cornerstone of human society is based on respect for the human nature. Our responsibility is not up in the sky. It is on earth. The Qur'an says ALLAH said, "*Get ye down from here into the earth, your place of livelihood and your place of resurrection.*"

CHAPTER 12

KA AND BA

The word Kaaba has several connotations. It refers to family connection or social unity. It means joints or joining together. The heavenly object connected with the earth which led to the construction of that Ancient House, the Kaaba. A house suggests home life and family. A family is a connection between people: husband, wife, children, uncle, aunt, et cetera. From the family comes the society which has more sophisticated connections. The Kaaba is the result of connections. It was built by joining bricks together, connecting horizontal lines with perpendicular lines. It requires the joining together of matter. This requires skill.

The emphasis on the Kaaba is actually emphasis on the family life and social order of man. That is why during the Hajj people from all over the world, from all different nationalities, come together---not to worship the House or themselves, but to worship the Lord of the House, ALLAH. The Qur'an says, "*Turn from where ever you are in the direction of that sacred house*", the Kab'ah. Once we understand the importance of that statement, we will not only turn in that direction physically, and respect that focal point and the physical structure, but we will turn towards our family and society wherever we are and show respect for our fellow human beings. Some people think it is okay to respect Western society but disrespect the African society, or the Chinese society, or the Arab society, et cetera. We are to respect and honor all good societies because each of them are connected one way or another.

The words Ka and Ba are also derived from an ancient Egyptian concept of the soul. The Africans of Egypt believed that the human being was not just physical, but that we are mental and spiritual as well. Their science of human nature and religion, therefore, focused on the connection between the present life and the life after death. The terms Ka and Ba were associated with the human being. They were connected to his physical life. However, upon the death of a person they (Ka and Ba) would separate and leave the body.

More specifically, the Ka was a term that referred to the creative and preserving power of life. It also alluded to intellectual and spiritual power that was born with each individual. According to some reports the Ka was closely associated with the physical or concrete matter. Remember, we said the word Kaaba meant connections. As evidence of this, we find that the Egyptian symbol of the Ka was two arms raised up to the sky. Each arm is joined or connected to the shoulder.

The Ba represented the soul or spiritual side of man. According to Egyptian mythology the Ba was originally only a part of the gods. It later was applied to all people. This happened at the end of the Old Kingdom. The Ka and the Ba were connected in the human being. Therefore, when we look in the direction of the Kaaba, the sacred House in Makkah, and consider the history and the wisdom that is associated with it, we will gain a greater appreciation for it as a symbol and a place of direction. The Kaaba represents the life and nature of man and society. The word Ba means soul. The Holy Qur'an says ALLAH created us from one soul (4:1) and then divided it into pairs. The Kaaba began with one stone, which is symbolic of the original nature in man. ALLAH said he made us from black clay. The black stone represents that black clay or original nature.

History tells us that there was a time when the Kaaba became corrupt and polluted with many idols. All kinds of indecent acts were performed around the Kaaba. History and present day reality shows us that man also has become corrupt and deviated from the proper path. Concerning the Kaaba as a sacred symbol in the life of man, Imam W. D. Muhammad explained very profoundly that, "Everyone of us in our own hearts and in our souls are a Kaaba. . . . All of us should have a sanctuary in here. We should reject bad things and keep it holy and safe. We should keep it secure. Then we would have a sense of health, a sense of soundness, a sense of well being, and a sense of safety. We will not fear everything. We will fear no other but God." (Newark, N.J. July 1988).

ALLAH tells us not to worship the Kaaba or ourselves, but to worship Him. The Holy Qur'an states, *"Let them adore the Lord of this House, Who provides them with food against hunger, and with security against fear (of danger)."* (106:3-4). Muslims make circles around the Kab'ah as a sign or symbol of the fact that the material matter is encompassed by God-consciousness or Taqwa. The circling of the Kaaba also refers to the importance of keeping our social and family life within the bounds of ALLAH'S (GOD'S) rule. The Kaaba is the most sacred House in the life of the Muslims. The Qur'an calls it the Ancient House. All Muslims must turn in that direction for prayer at least five times a day. It is a secure and respected place. It is essential for us to know the great value of the Kaaba in the life of Man. The religion of Al-Islam addresses every aspect in the life of man. All people can find their place of honor and dignity in Al-Islam.

CHAPTER 13

WE HELPED BUILD THE KAABA

The African Americans can find dignity and honor in the history of Al-Islam. Al-Islam is a universal religion. It embraces all people. There are those, however, who do not want man to have dignity and honor. The African people, for example, have been told that they were useless and inferior to every human being that walks the face of this earth. There seems to be an intentional conspiracy to hide the great role of the Black people of Africa in the development of civilization. The positive contributions that the Black Africans made to the world have been buried under the rubbish of racism, bigotry and jealousy. The only idea or ideology that can truly restore the lost history and worth of the African people in general, and the African American in particular, is Al-Islam.

The Holy Qur'an says Isma'il helped Abraham build the Kaaba in Makkah. Isma'il was the son of Abraham and a Black African woman from Egypt. It is a fact that our ancestor helped to build the most sacred place in the Islamic world and the life of man. ALLAH-U-AKBAR. We are not late comers to the religion of Al-Islam. We helped lay the foundation on Taqwa. This fact dispels the argument that Muslims enslaved Africans and made them accept Al-Islam. Abraham was the first conscious Muslim. The religion started with Abraham and was completed with Prophet Muhammad (PBUH). The African was there at the genesis and at the completion.

Bilal Ibn Rabah was a great help to Prophet Muhammad and the Religion of Islam. He was a Black man from Ethiopia. Those of us who are trying to help correct some of the wrongs of the past can point to the religion of Al-Islam as the solution for the ills of our people. Al-Islam does not only restore the ethnic heritage and honor of man, but it also restores his human excellence and motivates him to grow bigger than nationalism.

63

The African Americans have been deprived of their noble and honorable role in history. That must be restored! If our Ancestor was qualified enough in the sight of ALLAH (GOD) to help build the Holy Kaaba in Makkah, then surely we are qualified to read and study the Holy Qur'an and Sunnah of Prophet Muhammad for ourselves. One of the acts of Hajj is in commemoration of an event that occurred in the life of a Black African Women, from Egypt (Hagar). The African American needs to know that, we do not have to become an Arab, an Egyptian, a Pakistanian to be a Muslim. The only one that has a monopoly on this religion is ALLAH (GOD)!

The Holy Prophet Muhammad said, "he left us the Holy Qur'an and his Sunnah (way) and if we obey them we will never go astray". He did not say that he left us the Egyptian and the Iranian, or the Pakistanian and the Sudanese, and if we follow them we will never go astray. No! Modern history shows us that they have all strayed from the sober message of the Qur'an and the Sunnah.

The Prophet Muhammad (PBUH) said during his farewell address that there is no superiority of an Arab over a non-Arab, a Black over a White or a White over a Black.

CHAPTER 14

ABRAHAM: HOW WILL THE DEAD BE RAISED?

"Behold! Abraham said: "My Lord! Show me how Thou givest life to the dead." He said: Dost thou not then believe? He (Abraham) said: Yea! but to satisfy my own understanding. ALLAH said: Take four birds, tame them to turn to thee; Put a portion of them on every hill, and call to them: They will come to thee (Flying) with speed. Then know that ALLAH is Exalted in Power, Wise."
(H.Q. 2:260).

The above ayat contains a wealth of wisdom and an infinite degree of guidance for the life of man and society. Abraham inquired about the mystery of life and death. He believed that ALLAH (GOD) could and would give life to the dead, but he wanted a better understanding of it. He wanted to quench his curiosity. If we follow the way of Abraham with sincerity, then we will not be afraid to seek answers and question things that we may not understand. The response that Abraham got from ALLAH indicates that it is permitted for us to seek satisfaction for our hearts and minds.

One of the first things that we learn from the above ayat is that man is naturally curious. And that this tendency in man is approved by God as long as it is based on genuine sincerity and faith. It represents mental freedom. ALLAH did not tell Abraham that he was wrong to ask such a question. In fact, based on the answer that ALLAH gave Abraham, it suggests that He wanted Abraham to continue to think and reason. ALLAH prompted Abraham to dig deeper into the reservoir of his mind and analyze the creation and its relationship to man and God.

Prior to Abraham's inquiry about the resurrection, the Qur'an says that Iblis (Satan) also made a statement concerning the resurrection. Satan asked ALLAH, *"Give me respite till the day they are raised up." ALLAH said: "Be thou among those who have respite"* (7:14,15). Satan then responded by saying that he will attack the human being from four directions or situations. According to the Qur'an, Satan said, *"Then will I assault them from before them and behind them, from their right and their left... "* (7:17). Satan launched a universal plot on the human being. He covered the four bases or aspects of human life. He said he would assault us from the front (before). He is an open enemy to man. "Before" us, means open, outright oppression of the human life. He said he would come from behind. This refers to his secret whispers and hidden suggestions. Assaulting us from the right means Satan will come at us from our strong position of faith. He tries to make our stronger, righteous position a burden on us so that we will become weak and give up. The left means that he will appeal to our weakness, our faults.

Returning to Abraham, we find that he was directed towards four also. ALLAH told him to train four birds and then place them on four mountains or hills. To train or tame is to establish a pattern of discipline. Man does not teach birds to fly; that is their nature. Men train birds how to obey them. Abraham taught four birds how to obey him. Birds represent an ability to rise above the material or physical desires. Their strongest senses are sight and hearing. Abraham was told to tame the birds, place them on four mountains and then call them. Each prophet or messenger was a caller. Each prophet beckoned man and society to return back to the right path. Satan approached man from four sides and he said he would break or destroy the natural discipline in us to obey ALLAH (GOD). According to the Qur'an he said he would do this until the day we were raised. Once we are disciplined to the point where we can hear and obey the call of righteousness and intelligent reasoning, we will regain the life that ALLAH intended for us. ALLAH gives life to the dead by restoring the discipline and obedient nature in us. Four represents universality: north, east, south and west. The Qur'an says ALLAH will bring about a complete resurrection of all humanity.

66

If Satan said he would deceive or assault man from four directions or positions, then it should follow that the righteous appeal to man should be made from four positions or directions. ALLAH did not leave Satan alone to do whatever he wanted to without a fight. Just as there are wicked people all over the world, there are righteous people all over the world.

The Qur'an also says ALLAH provided us with nourishment in four days. (41:10). And the Qur'an says Satan threatens us with "poverty and want". We can understand Abraham calling the four birds to mean that, if we train and discipline our spirit on this material earth (mountains or hills) to obey the command of ALLAH (GOD), then Satan's open plot or secret plans will not destroy us. Nor would his scheme to assault us from our position of weakness or strength. ALLAH (GOD) will show Satan, that everywhere on this earth where he has caused death, destruction and corruption, ALLAH (GOD) will give life and raise the dead. We see, for example, here in America where the enemies of humanity thought they had successfully destroyed any idea of Islam among the African American, but ALLAH (GOD) has raised up a dead community to life in response to the call of ALLAH (GOD), through the Qur'an and the Sunnah of Prophet Muhammad (PBUH). Actually this is happening in the four corners of the world. The Muslim community is coming back to life. The response that ALLAH (GOD) gave Abraham requires us to think and ponder. ALLAH (GOD) could have given Abraham a very simple demonstration. He could have told Abraham to go to the nearest grave yard and observe a dead body come to life. Or He could have drawn Abraham's attention to the trees to show how they die in the winter and come back to life in the spring. ALLAH (GOD) chose to use birds, mountains, a human being and a call (the voice) to demonstrate how He gives life to the dead. Think!

Abraham had already demonstrated that he was a man of faith and reason. He had already shown that he could reason logically and arrive at intelligent conclusions. Some people you have to give them simple direct answers. Some people you have to show pictures and simple example. Other people may require a more complex or sophisticated answer. The human being does not grasp knowledge in the same way. That is why there are various methods of teaching. ALLAH (GOD) uses different ways of attracting our attention in the Qur'an. The Qur'an gives us simple parables as well as complex and sophisticated parables. In fact, it uses different parables to give the same message. (H. Q. 39:27)

If we think about it, the answer that was given to Abraham required him to think. Abraham had wisdom. The Qur'an says ALLAH (GOD) *"granted wisdom to whom he pleaseth; and he to whom wisdom is granted receiveth indeed a benefit overflowing; But none will grasp the Message but men of understanding."* (2:269).

Abraham was told to tame the four birds first. To tame is to teach or educate. This brings to mind the idea of dawah. The Prophet Muhammad said, "it is best to teach one hour of the night, than it is to pray all night." Prior to this event, the Qur'an tells us that Abraham was ordered to build the Kaaba which is a square or a four pointed figure. Most buildings are laid on a four pointed foundation. Therefore, four refers to the beginning or origin. It alludes to the starting point. The human being starts out on four as a baby. We can reason then that the four birds alluded to the original nature of man. The human being was taken away from his original nature of excellence and goodness. We were originally created in Deen-Al-Fitr. Our resurrection will come about by being re-acquainted with our original nature. Once we are taught and trained to obey the natural call of our creation and organize it, we will return to it immediately. The Qur'an says The birds will *"come to thee (flying) with speed."* The Qur'an also says the believers say, *"We hear and we obey."*

Abraham was told to place the four birds on four hills or mountains. Our original nature is both physical and spiritual. ALLAH (GOD) says if He had revealed the Qur'an on a mountain, it would have crumbled, but He revealed it on the heart of a human being, Prophet Muhammad (PBUH). Although it was revealed on his heart, it did not just stay there, in fact it changed the whole physical and spiritual life of the Arabs and most of the then known world.

Let us consider the fact that four disciplined birds were placed on four material mountains or hills. The Qur'an says, "*And We have set on the earth mountains standing firm...*" (21:31). Birds are a symbol of spiritual discipline, and mountains or hills represent material growth and development. Our material life should always be ruled over by spiritual discipline. If not, we may become selfish, greedy, materialistic and immoral. Once our heart and spirit is attuned to the call of righteousness our life can be restored.

The physical creation is composed of four basic elements: earth, water, fire and air. Each of these elements are needed for life. The calling together or union of these elements brings life to man and creation as a whole. These elements also have spiritual and symbolic meaning in the life of man. As I have explained in my other works, Earth alludes to the material nature; water represents moral vision and communication; fire refers to wisdom; and air symbolizes spiritual activity. If we don't attend to these four aspects in the proper way, they can become inactive and die. Or, if ALLAH (GOD) wills, they can die. However, if they are trained through prayer to obey the command of ALLAH (GOD), they can become active again. The Qur'an says ALLAH (GOD) can bring about a total resurrection. It says He can resurrect us to our very finger tips. Therefore, if we die physically (earth), morally (water), intellectually (fire), and/or spiritually (air), He can call us back to our original form.

This lets us know also that if the man who stands on the mountain of material success, or the man who stands on the mountain of moral excellence, and/or the man who stands on the hill or mountain of wisdom, or the man who stands on the hill of spiritual vision and activity, should die or deviate from the proper course, that ALLAH (GOD) can call them back to life again.

The Qur'an does not tell us how Abraham called the birds. We don't know if he whistled, or if he said "come in the name of

ALLAH (GOD)", or if he called them with his hand. What we do know is that Abraham did call them. As Muslims we receive a call five times each and every day. The adhan is called in each corner of the earth and it beckons us to come to prayer, spiritual (life) and cultivation (mental and physical life). The believer who has disciplined his life to respond to the adhan, awakes each morning from his sleep (which is a minor form of death) and responds to the call to prayer. In fact, when the adhan is called all of the Muslims turn in one direction, towards the Kaaba that was built by Abraham. The birds returned to one direction, towards Abraham. It can be reasoned, logically and philosophically, that Abraham calling the birds, or four positions of the birds, relates to the Muslim community responding to the call to prayer. Abraham was a human being, yet he was told to call birds, not another human being.

The adhan is actually a call to the entire creation. ALLAH has placed man in charge of the creation. The Qur'an says Allah made us his vicegerent (2:39, 6:165) therefore we are responsible for the up keep of creation. The Qur'an says corruption has appeared on the land and the sea because of what man has done. ALLAH (GOD) blessed the Muslims to come up with a call that is made by the human voice and not by some other instrument. The adhan goes to the very core and essence of creation.

CHAPTER 15

THE SIGNIFICANCE OF THE ADHAN

The Muslim man calls the creation to prayer. We believe, based on the Qur'an and the words of Prophet Muhammad (PBUH), that the whole creation is Muslim. Every Muslim is required to respond to the adhan. If a Muslim is placed out in the desert, the jungle, or the wilderness all alone, no human life anywhere in sight, he still calls the adhan. Why? Because it is not just for his Muslim brother but for the Muslim creation. The adhan starts with four definitive statements: ALLAHU-AKBAR (GOD is Greater). Abraham took four birds and placed them on four hills or mountains. So we start our day by saying or hearing that ALLAH is greater than everything, four times. The Qur'an says ALLAH (GOD) gave the creation the nourishment in four periods. Well, ALLAH is greater than that. ALLAH is greater than the man in the north, east, south or west. ALLAH is greater than the four basic elements: earth, water, fire and air. He is greater than the material, the moral, the intellectual and the spiritual aspects of life. ALLAH is greater than the tetragrammaton (Yod-He-Vau-He).

Although the Adhan is generally defined as the Muslim call to prayer, only certain aspects of it are actually a call. The first part, ALLAHU-AKBAR (God is Greater), is an objective and definitive statement (four times). The second and third part is a subjective declaration based on knowledge: "I bear witness there is no god but ALLAH" (twice). "I bear witness that Muhammad is the Messenger of ALLAH" (twice). The fourth and fifth parts are calls to action. "Come to prayer" (twice) "Come to success or cultivation" (twice). At the sixth part we return to the original statement: ALLAHU-AKBAR (twice). The seventh part is said only once: "There is no god but ALLAH."

on the earth and measured therein all things to give them nourishment in due proportion, in four days, in accordance with (the needs of) those who seek (sustenance). (41:10)

The adhan is divided into fours, twos and one. If we think about it, it actually ties in with what the Qur'an says of man and creation. As I stated earlier, the Qur'an mentions four days (41:10). ALLAH also says He made us in twos. The Qur'an says ALLAH "has created pairs in all things" (43:12). "And of every thing We have created pairs: That ye may receive instruction." (50:49). The Qur'an also explains how ALLAH (GOD) created the human being in twains and then scattered us throughout the earth (4:1). ALLAH has made us male and female. The creation consists of positive and negative, good and bad, light and darkness, left and right, strength and weakness, conscious and subconscious. We have two eyes, two ears, two arms, two legs, two lips, two nostrils, etc. ALLAH also says there are two easts and two wests "he is Lord of the two Easts and Lord of the two Wests" (55:17).

It can be reasoned that the part of the adhan that is said twice addresses the duality of man and nature. However, the destiny is towards oneness, Tawheed. The last part of the adhan is one statement: "There is no god but ALLAH." After we go through our four and two stages, we return to one creation. The last statement of the adhan brings us back to the "ultimate reality." All Muslims turn in one direction, towards the Kaaba. ALLAH (GOD) says our death and resurrection is as one soul. He also says we are created from a single person (39:6). The Creator has given us only one heart and one head. In fact, every member of our body works for the benefit or harm of the whole. The destiny of the universe is towards oneness. We are one humanity from one creation. ALLAH (GOD) is One. When man arrives at the great wisdom of human nature and then sees or realizes that his lord is one, that his total allegiance should only be given to one God, he will then be ready to serve Him. "There is no god but ALLAH" ends the adhan. "After that we prepare for prayer. That call sets man into action. It awakens the nature of man and creation, and it reminds him of his obligations.

lord is one, that his total allegiance should only be given to one God, he will then be ready to serve Him. "There is no god but ALLAH" ends the adhan. "After that we prepare for prayer. That call sets man into action. It awakens the nature of man and creation, and it reminds him of his obligations.

The adhan is a complete address to man and society. It reaches the total man. The adhan is divided into seven parts. Seven represents completion. Brothers and Sisters, we must understand that the knowledge is connected because it come from one source. Think about this! The adhan has seven parts, the most important and often said prayer consists of seven ayats. It is a complete prayer. In fact it is the essence of the Qur'an (15:87). There are seven levels of heaven and earth (65:12); seven gates of hell. Hagar ran seven times between Safa and Mawah; Prophet Muhammad ascended to the seventh heaven. During Hajj Muslims walk around the Kab'ah seven times. There are seven days in a week.

The adhan is the most significant call in the Muslim life because it does not only call the Muslims to a ritual of prayer, but it actually calls the entire creation to the remembrance of ALLAH (GOD). It also reminds us of our unity with creation as well as our responsibility to God, to ourselves, and to society. Reflect!

Let us consider this: The Muslim hears the adhan which consists of seven parts. He hears this seven days a week. Each time he turns in the direction of the Kaaba, which he is required to go around seven times (during Hajj). Then he recites a seven part prayer (Al-Fatiha). At the end of the salat, the Muslims ask ALLAH (GOD) to bless Muhammad, who ascended to the seventh heaven, and we mention Abraham who was also on the seventh heaven. We also stand upon the earth which has seven levels. The Qur'an says, "*And We have bestowed upon thee the Seven Oft-repeated (verses) and the Grand Qur'an.*"(15:87). In Surah 65, Ayat 12 it states, "*God is He Who created seven firmaments and of the earth a similar number.*" ALLAHU-AKBAR!

(Revelation 5:1-4). Al-Fatiha represents the opening of the seven seals, and the sharing of the sacred knowledge. The Prophet Muhammad's ascension to the seventh heaven also represents the completion and fulfillment of the destiny of man, and the unfolding of the truth of the prophets. Prior to Prophet Muhammad, the life of the previous prophets were concealed under lies and mis-conception. Just as there are seven levels of heaven or paradise there are also seven gates of hell. (15:44).

Another way of looking at the adhan, is as a call to education and refinement of the human senses. The human being is composed of three aspects; physical, mental and spiritual. Each of these aspects need refinement and direction. Our five senses evolve on all three levels. In our physical body they are sight, smell, hearing, taste and feeling. Mentally they evolve to what we call reason, insight, sensitivity, wisdom, etc. Spiritually the senses are related to intuition. The Qur'an says, "*ye shall surely travel from stage to stage.*" (84:19). Five senses on three levels, equal fifteen. The adhan consists of fifteen expressions. The adhan addresses the total being. It addresses us physically, mentally and spiritually. When the Muezzin makes the call to prayer, he makes fifteen expressions. God is Greater (4 times); I bear witness there is no god but ALLAH (2 times); I bear witness that Muhammad is His Messenger (2 times); Come to Prayer (2 times); come to success (2 times) God is Greater (2 times). There is no god but ALLAH (1 time). We get $4 + 2 + 2 + 2 + 2 + 2 + 1$ =15. Our religion consists of five pillars, five prayers, five times a day. This world needs to hear the Adhan because it has failed to address all of the needs of the human being.

ABRAHAM, ISMAIL, PROPHET MUHAMMAD AND BILAL

After Abraham and Isma'il built the Kaaba for all of humanity, it later became corrupted with idols. This sacred Shrine became filled with idols. The pagan Arabs, during their time of ignorance, disrespected this holy sanctuary. History tells us however, that with the advent of Prophet Muhammad, the Kaaba was restored. The Kaaba in Makkah is the most sacred and honored place for the Muslims. According to history, when the

Prophet Muhammad and his followers returned to Makkah victoriously, he ordered Bilal Ibn Rabah to stand on the top of the Kaaba and call the Adhan. That was a powerful message.

Bilal was a former slave. Prophet Muhammad did not only choose this Black African form Ethiopia to be the first Muezzin (Prayer Caller), but he directed him to stand upon the sacred house and make the call. Prophet Muhammad (PBUH), a free man, told an ex-slave to stand upon a house that was built by the first conscious Muslim, Abraham and the son (Isma'il) of a black slave women named, Hagar. Standing on the Kaaba suggests that we should stand upon that which is sacred. If we stand upon the sacred word of ALLAH (GOD) and this sacred religion, then we will be above the world. What did Bilal do? He made that great call to humanity. We should not aspire to be above people so that we can oppress them. The position and responsibility of leadership is to direct and guide the people towards truth.

Oh ALLAH! exalt Muhammad and the followers of Muhammad as Thou did exalt Abraham and the followers of Abraham. And bless Muhammad and the followers of Muhammad as Thou did bless Abraham and the followers of Abraham, verily Thou art praiseworthy, and glorious.

BIBLIOGRAPHY

1. Holy Qur'an, Yusuf Ali Translation

2. Holy Bible, King James Version

3. The Bible, The Qur'an and Science, Maurice Bucaille, Paris, France 1982

4. Al-Islam, Christianity and Freemasonry, Mustafa El-Amin, New Mind Productions, 1985

5. Freemasonry, Ancient Egypt, and the Islamic Destiny, Mustafa El-Amin, New Mind Productions, 1988

6. Prayer and Al-Islam, Imam Warithuddin Muhammad, Muhammad Islamic Foundation, Chicago, Illinois, 1982

7. An African-American Genesis, W. Deen Muhammad, M.A.C.A. Publications Calumet City, Illinois, 1986

8. Democracy Is Self Government, H.W. Percival, The Word Publishing Co., 1952

9. Muhammad Encyclopedia of Seerah, Vol. I Afzal Ur Rahman, The Muslim School Trust, London, England, 1981

10. World's Great Men of Color, J.A. Rogers, MacMillan Publishing Co., Inc., 1972

11. The Destruction of Black Civilization, Chancellor Williams, Third World Press, 1976

12. From Babylon to Timbuktu, Rudolph R. Windsor, Exposition Press, New York, 1976

13. Towards Understanding Islam, A. Maududi

14. <u>Closing of The American Mind</u>, Allan Bloom,
    Simon and Schuster, New York, 1987

15. <u>What Every American Should Know About Islam and The
    Muslims,</u> Muhammad Armiya Nu'Man, New Mind
    Productions, Jersey City, 1985

16. <u>Evolution of Religion Through The Prophets</u>, Muhammad
    Armiya Nu'Man, New Mind Productions, 1979

BIOGRAPHY

Mustafa El-Amin was born in Newark, New Jersey on November 13, 1957. He received a B.A. Degree in Community Development from Rutgers University, New Brunswick, New Jersey in 1979. In 1983, he received a Masters Degree in Public Administration.

Mr. El-Amin has also written other major works, "LET THERE BE LIGHT" published in 1981, "AL-ISLAM, CHRISTIANITY, AND FREEMASONRY" published in 1985, and "FREEMASONRY, ANCIENT EGYPT AND THE ISLAMIC DESTINY" published in 1988.

If you have comments or suggestions on this or other works by this author, you may forward them to: El-Amin Productions, P.O. Box 32148, Newark, N.J. 07102.

Also, Mustafa El-Amin is available for public speaking engagements, workshops and/or seminars. Send requests and inquiries to El-Amin Productions, P.O. Box 32148, Newark, N.J. 07102.

THINK! THINK!! THINK!!!

"The Arabic word "iman" which we have translated into English as "faith" literally means 'to know, to believe, and to be convinced beyond a shadow of a doubt!'...Thus, faith is firm belief arising out of knowledge and conviction."

Abraham is an example of the rational urge in man. Although he was a Prophet and the first conscious Muslim, he can also be seen as a model of what occurs in the human being...Allah says in the Qur'an that it is *He* who brings man from darkness to light.

We too, like Abraham, may have looked at three things (Mother, Father and Society) because of their role in our life and because at certain points in our growth they were 'the greater'. That natural process creates in us a sense of appreciation so that once we come to know the real God, we will already know how to show appreciation towards Him.

FREEMASONRY

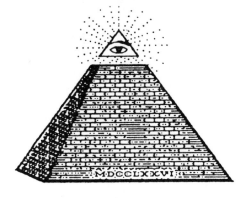

ANCIENT EGYPT

And The

ISLAMIC DESTINY

$6.95 +
1.25 Shipping

By Mustafa El-Amin

What Every American Should Know About Islam & The Muslims

● by Imam Muhammad Armiya Nu'Man ●

$5.00 +
1.25 Shipping

Al-Islam

Christianity

&

Freemasonry

by Mustafa El-Amin

$7.95 +
1.25 Shipping

The Evolution of Religion Through The Prophets

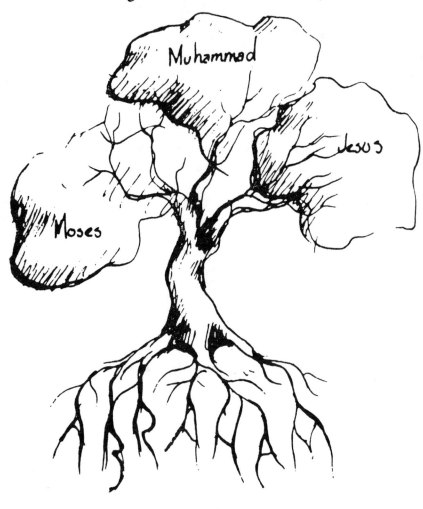

By Muhammad Armiya Nu'Man

$2.75 +
1.00 Shipping

بِسْمِ اللهِ الرَّحْمَانِ الرَّحِيمِ

MUSLIM - MASONIC DIALOGUE

On Video

FEATURING

MUSTAFA EL-AMIN,
AUTHOR OF BOOK, "AL-ISLAM, CHRISTIANITY & FREEMASONRY"

AND

REV. ROBERT L. UZZEL OF THE PHYLAXIS SOCIETY-PRINCE HALL MASONS' 14th ANNUAL SESSION

ORDER YOURS TODAY!!!

VIDEO $25.00 + $1.50 FOR POSTAGE
AUDIO CASSETTE ALSO AVAILABLE, ONLY $5.00
BOOK: "Al-Islam, Christianity, & Freemasonry" Only $6.95 + $1.00 Pstg.

MAIL TO NEW MIND PRODUCTIONS, P. O. BOX 5185, JERSEY CITY, NJ 07305

NAME_____

ADDRESS_____

CITY_____STATE_____ZIP_____

NOTES